HUNTING, FISHING AND CAMPING

HUNTING FISHING
— and —
CAMPING

by

Leon Leonwood Bean

with Updates by Great-Grandson

Bill Gorman

100TH ANNIVERSARY EDITION

L.L.Bean

— FREEPORT, MAINE —

Copyright © 2011 L.L. Bean
All rights reserved
ISBN 978-1-60893-012-8
Design by Miroslaw Jurek

Printed in China
5   4   3   2   1

Down East
Books · Magazine · Online
Rockport, Maine
www.downeast.com

Distributed to the trade by National Book Network

Library of Congress Cataloging-in-Publication Data

Bean, L. L. (Leon Leonwood), 1872-1966.
Hunting, fishing, and camping / by Leon Leonwood Bean ; with updates & notes by Bill Gorman,
great-grandson of L.L. Bean. -- 100th anniversary ed.
p. cm.
ISBN 978-1-60893-012-8
1. Hunting. 2. Fishing. 3. Camping. I. Title.
SK33.B42 2012
799.2--dc23
2011036111

The author with a
salmon taken on live
bait-fly as described
on page 50.

A Note from Bill Gorman

As a boy, I always looked forward to visiting my great-grandfather L.L. at his retail store in Freeport. In my eyes, he was a strong, smiling man with a big personality presiding over a boy's dream — a world of mesmerizing animal mounts, tents, axes, sleeping bags, and fishing rods. Although he died when I was only five years old, L.L. has been a powerful influence in shaping who I am today. The joy I receive from hunting, fishing, and just being outdoors is his legacy to me.

My great-grandfather was an astute entrepreneur and an eminently practical man, but he was, above all else, a passionate outdoorsman. That blend of passion and practicality is what led him to write his *Hunting Fishing and Camping* guide, which he said should be readable in eighty-five minutes. His point, after all, was not to immerse his audience in tales of the outdoors, but in the outdoors itself.

I would, however, suggest spending a little bit longer enjoying this edition of L.L.'s classic. First published in 1942, *Hunting Fishing and Camping* has lost some of its practical use as a hands-on manual in this twenty-first-century age of Gore-Tex rainwear and graphite fly rods (although a surprising amount of its advice still holds up today). But as a nostalgic look at a bygone era in the Maine woods, this book knows no equal. That's one of the reasons we have decided to bring it back into print, with updated information about the ways our favorite outdoor pursuits have changed since L.L.'s day — and the ways they have stayed the same.

In many ways, too, L.L. Bean has changed since my great-grandfather was at the helm. While it is a much bigger company with a far broader line of products, L.L.'s influence endures in our legendary commitment to customer service. And today's L.L.Bean actively promotes the responsible use of the outdoors that L.L.

so deeply loved, through sustainable forest management, energy conservation, green building design, and use of alternative energy, as well as charitable support for conservation and outdoor recreation organizations.

Of course, the best way to convince people of the importance of conservation is to take them hunting, fishing, or camping, as my great-grandfather understood. L.L. introduced generations to the pleasures of experiencing nature firsthand. In his original introduction to this book, L.L. wrote that "venturing into the great open spaces... teaches us to forget the mean and petty things of life." That is a lesson whose value has only increased with time.

— Bill Gorman, 2012

L.L. Bean, the author,
of Freeport, Maine,
and moose shot by
him in fall of 1935.

Introduction

The object of this book is not to bore my readers with personal yarns and experiences but to give definite information in the fewest words possible on how to Hunt, Fish, and Camp.

I am confining the territory to Maine, however, the same instructions and rules apply to all sections of the country where the same fish and game are found.

To make this book as brief as possible, I am dealing only with major information. Minor details are easily learned by practice. The instructions are so condensed that the reading time of the whole book is only 85 minutes.

If you have youngsters coming on, let them read this book. The information is just as important as many school text books.

I am a firm believer in the conservation of all fish and game and the strict enforcement of all game laws. To my mind, hunting and fishing is the big lure that takes us into the great open spaces and teaches us to forget the mean and petty things of life.

— Leon Leonwood Bean, 1942

I desire to acknowledge with appreciation the valued cooperation of:

The Maine Forestry Department

Warden Supervisor Arthur Rogers

Henry Milliken

Henry Beverage

George Soule

O.H.P. Rodman

J. Larry Hawkes

Parker Foss

Guy Bean

L.L. Bean's Duck Hunting
Camp at Merrymeeting Bay
near Brunswick, Maine.

Table of Contents

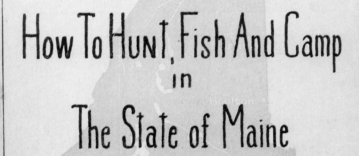

How To Hunt, Fish And Camp

in

The State of Maine

BY

L. L. Bean

Freeport   Maine

CHAPTER 1

Deer Hunting on Bare Ground

The first thing to decide: Where shall I go? Second: How many do I want to make up the party?

Where to go is the most important question to settle. You will find your answer on page 86.

Now for your party. A perfect trip may be ruined by one person who does not fit. I recommend small parties, not over four. Two makes a good party. »

The next thing after making up your party and where to go is to decide on your camp. Shall you use a tent, a lean-to, an old logging camp or go to a regular Sporting camp?

A Sporting camp is the most comfortable and the least trouble, but sometimes the hunting is not so good on account of too many hunters. »

Next is your equipment and what to wear—you will find your answers to both these questions on pages 37, 39 and 40.

Now that you are settled in camp, each hunter should look over safety rules and make a copy of signals in Chapter 14.

The next question is: How are you going to hunt? With a small party I recommend still hunting as driving is out of the question. I realize that driving is fairly successful in the Southern States but not in Maine. I have found still hunting the most successful method on both bare ground and snow. Early in the season you stand a chance to get a good shot near camp. The best hunting is early in the morning, regardless of the season. The first thing to do is to find out the direction of the wind. Travel with the wind in your face. Walk slowly, stop often, take in all the territory around you and always be in position to shoot quickly.

Watch for fresh signs and try to follow the way you are going but always keep the wind in your face, if possible.

Do not hunt too long the first day or two. Start back to camp by 10:00 o'clock. The middle of the day is the poorest time to hunt. If you find fresh signs near camp go out again about 2:00 o'clock and sit down in a place where you have a good view and an open place to shoot. »

BILL GORMAN
« *Two made a good hunting party in the past when you depended on a partner to know where you were and to help drag animals out. Nowadays, with cell phones and better communication, you can more easily hunt solo.*

BILL GORMAN
« *If you want to hunt from a sporting camp, choose one whose operators are sensitive to scent. It's nice to wake up to bacon and eggs, but you don't want to smell like bacon and eggs during your hunt. Look for lodges whose facilities for preparing and serving meals are separate from those where you keep your clothes.*

BILL GORMAN
« *Our concept of time certainly has changed. In L.L.'s day, outdoorsmen hunted for days at a time. Today, we're lucky if we can hunt for a few hours. I love hunting in early morning and early evening, but if my time is limited, I'll hunt whenever I can.*

If it is a beech-nut year you will do well to put in a lot of time on the beech ridges. You are very likely to find where deer have pawed over the beech leaves looking for nuts. Walk very slowly along where you can see quite a distance. If it is a bright, clear day keep near the edge of the ridge where the hard wood and black growth meet. If you find fresh signs sit down where you can see some distance looking into the wind. If you are not sure of the direction of the wind wet your finger in your mouth and hold it over your head. The side that feels cold is where the wind is coming from.

If there are no beechnuts look for signs on burned ground and where lumbermen have operated. Deer browse on small hard wood shoots and raspberry bushes. Whenever you find signs keep a sharp lookout and step where you will not break twigs. Deer's eyesight is poor but their sense of hearing and smelling is very keen. They are apt to scent or hear you and be off before you see them.

If you wound a deer and find blood do not rush him. Signal your partner. Sit down and wait for the deer to lie down and stiffen up. If in the afternoon, however, get him before you are obliged to leave for camp if possible as it may storm during the night and obliterate the trail. »

Above: Lyman Lane, age 10, of East Swanzey, N.H. shot this deer with his Father's 30-30 rifle at 8:30 A.M., December 13, 1950, just before going to school. Lyman has been well trained in the use of a rifle and is an excellent marksman. He dropped the deer at a distance of about 200 yards. He also shot a doe on the second day of the hunting season 1951. Again in 1952 Lyman shot a deer on the last day of the season. Therefore at the age of twelve, he has to his credit three deer, which is an unusual record.

— CHAPTER 2 —

Deer Hunting on Snow

Strike out, taking your easy walking gait, until you hit a fresh track. Walk right along on it until it begins to zig-zag, then you must stop, look and listen. Mr. Deer is looking for a place to lie down. Now start hunting in earnest. Walk slowly and always be in a position to shoot. See that there is no snow in your sights or in your gun barrel.

If you get a standing shot, take a very careful aim at the fore shoulder if possible.

Should you suddenly come on to running tracks you can walk as fast as you like until deer starts walking again. Then slow down and watch for zig-zag tracks. Always keep a sharp lookout on both sides of tracks as occasionally other deer come in from the side.

If a deer starts browsing note the direction of the wind. If the wind is not in your face, start circling so as to bring it in your face. Because you are wasting your time by following a deer that can scent you before you see him. »

For successful hunting the snow should be soft, dry and fluffy. If the snow is crunchy under your feet or is frozen and crusted, it is worse than no snow at all for good deer hunting.

It takes a little practice to determine the difference between fresh tracks

BILL GORMAN

« *The biggest deer I've seen in my life was in Maine. He probably had a live weight of 290 pounds or better, and his antlers were so big they looked like arms coming out of his head. I was bow hunting and I had him at fifteen yards, but I didn't feel 100 percent confident about my shot due to obstructions, so I let him walk. To this day, I know it was the right thing to do.*

BILL GORMAN

« *Knowing your wind direction is still the best advice for dealing with scent. We can do whatever we can to de-scent ourselves (special clothing, breath sprays, etc.), but the most important thing is facing the wind, whether you are tracking deer or hunting from a tree stand. Set up multiple tree stands, so you have options depending on which way the wind is blowing.*

BILL GORMAN

» *I'd like to be able to track deer on bare snow, but I don't have the time. Today the majority of successful hunters use tree stands. Place tree stands close to where the deer are eating, bedding, or rutting. I try to find where their trails converge because I double my chances.*

and old tracks, but if snow falls during the night and you are out early in the morning it is fairly certain that you will strike fresh track if there are deer in the vicinity. «

— CHAPTER 3 —

How to Dress a Deer

First swing him around so that his head will hang over a small log or nubble with hind quarters down hill. Spread his hind legs well apart, make a careful incision in the belly right where it curves up from the legs, cutting through the skin and the very thin layer covering the paunch. Remembering that the hide and membrane is very thin here and that you do not want to cut into the paunch. Place the point of your knife between the first two fingers of your left hand, so that the back of the hand will press the paunch down and the point of the knife will cut the skin. Cut forward until you have an opening from twelve to fifteen inches long. Roll up both sleeves above the elbow, insert both hands, one on each side of the paunch, well forward and roll it out through the opening. Do not make this opening any larger than is necessary in order to do this. The bowels and liver will follow the paunch. Now reach way forward with your right hand and you will strike a membranous wall. Puncture this with your fingers and on the other side you will find his heart and lungs. Reach beyond this and cut windpipe with jackknife. Now pull out the heart and lungs and you have a deer that is known as "woods dressed." It is not necessary to cut the throat to bleed him. In most cases all the blood will escape through the shot hole. If not, the dressing operation will bleed him thoroughly. It is a good idea to remove the end of the intestine at the rectum. By doing this you will make a drain. By drawing a small bough through this hole all the blood will drain out. »

BILL GORMAN
« *Open up your deer and remove the hide as soon as possible to let the animal cool down. Take care to keep the hide and hair separate from the meat. These measures will preserve the meat's flavor.*

— CHAPTER 4 —

How to Hang up a Deer

If a small one you will have no trouble as you can tie your drag line around his neck, throw the loose end over the limb of a tree and pull him clear of the ground.

If a big deer, find a sapling that can be pulled over, so that, you can hitch your line to it high enough, so that, when it springs back it will lift the carcass from the ground. In case the "spring back" is not enough, use a pole with crotch or fork at end to prop it back in place. In some cases

Left: Showing how one man can hang up a large deer.

BILL GORMAN

» *Don't let your deer hang for more than a day. Get it into a cooler and then to a butcher as soon as possible.*

two poles are much better than one. Now sign and detach a tag from your hunting license and fasten it to the deer.

If deer is hung in the open, arrange black growth boughs, so the sun will not shine on it. If in fly time use an inexpensive cotton deer bag with puckering string that closes bag tight around the neck. If weather is warm get it into cold storage as soon as possible. A lot of game is spoiled every year before it reaches the table.

The next thing is to spot (blaze) trees and bushes from where it is hung to the nearest travelled trail or stream that leads to camp. «

Right: Fill out the tag that is attached to your hunting license and fasten it to your deer. In Maine, deer may be confiscated if not properly tagged.

Do not depend on your memory as to where the deer is hung. Many a deer has never been found after it was hung up. Should you employ a guide, he will do all this work, but, in place of a gun insist that he take along a medium size axe, a small camp kit with tea and lunch enough for 36 hours, (see Chapter 38). If you want to get pictures have him take along a camera. Your own rifle is enough but if you want to get partridge he can take along your light shot gun.

The most difficult and back-breaking task connected with deer hunting is the process of transporting a deer to camp. If the deer is small and there is snow on the ground, you can do fairly well by fastening a rope to the neck or antlers of the deer and attaching the loose end to a piece of sapling about 1 ½ inches in diameter and six inches long, using the sapling as a handle. If you have a companion, use a handle two feet in length.

If a big deer use a one wheel deer carrier or hire someone with a horse.

Dragging a big buck on bare ground for several miles is a task that you will long remember. Get all the members of your party to help you.

If you kill a deer "way back" and deer carrier is not available and you can hire someone with a horse to transport it to camp, you certainly are in luck, because the few dollars that you spend for toting will save you much hard labor.

If you are obliged to get your deer out on bare ground, without a horse or a deer carrier, use two poles. Tie deer well up between them. You will find this much better than one pole as it eliminates all the disagreeable "slat" or swinging. »

BILL GORMAN
« *In Maine, hunters prize body weight almost as much as a nice set of antlers. Hunters who harvest a deer with a minimum dressed weight of 200 pounds are eligible for the Biggest Bucks in Maine Club, sponsored by the* Maine Sportsman *magazine. I'm not a member of the 200 club yet: the biggest deer I've shot in Maine weighed 175 pounds.*

CHAPTER 5

How to Hunt Black Bear

No game animal in Maine is more elusive, more difficult to stalk, or once having been started, more difficult to shoot than a black bear. A bear is seldom caught unawares, for he has an almost uncanny sense of smell and is faster than chain lightning in his mental and physical reactions.

In northern Maine the best month to hunt black bear is October, for it is the month that they are locating comfortable winter quarters and are intent on piling on surplus fat in anticipation of a long sleep to come.

If the beechnuts are plentiful, walk slowly along the hardwood ridges, not on top of the ridges, but where the black growth mingles with the hardwoods. Travel with wind in your face. Be on alert. Should the bear you are hunting smell or hear you, he certainly will head for parts unknown without any preliminary motions. He won't stop to investigate, and once started, you might as well find a needle in a haystack as to attempt to locate him that day.

Below: Quadruplet Cub Bears found by a guide in Jackman, Maine, June 1950. The old bear was shot and the cubs went up a tree. To my knowledge, this is the only case on record of four cubs in one litter.

If you find the leaves of beech trees in small stacks or windrows and signs look fresh, sit down in a well hidden spot and keep on the lookout. Stay there a half-hour or so and then proceed on your way along the edge of the same ridge. Look carefully at the "black stumps" as you walk along, for occasionally these "stumps" are black bears.

If there is any place where there has been a forest fire and consequently acres of blackened trees and stumps, walk along the edge of places. Bears like to explore for grubs and you may see one ripping a stump apart for just such morsels.

One of the most successful bear hunters in Maine confines his activities to the vicinity of lumber camps. The place where the camp's gar-

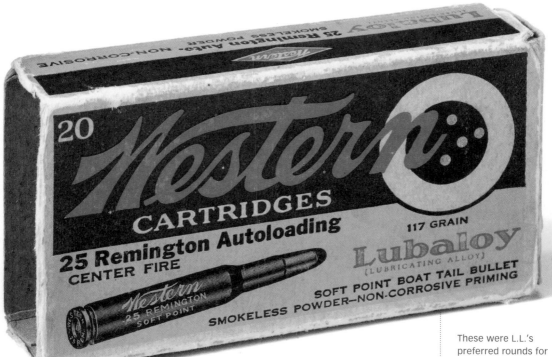

These were L.L.'s preferred rounds for use with his Remington autoloading rifle. Now obsolete, this caliber would have been best suited for small to medium game, but could have been used for something bigger in a pinch.

bage is thrown away is carefully looked over. If signs denote that bears make frequent forage on the garbage the hunter climbs into a tree near the spot and awaits the visit of Bruin. He hunts only in the afternoon, climbing into his tree perch about two o'clock and staying there until dark.

Bears like to walk up and down old tote and logging roads, so saunter along slowly and sit down occasionally—and trust to luck. Black bear hunting is mostly a matter of luck anyway. You may hunt for twenty years and not catch sight of one, or you may see one the first day on a hardwood ridge.

You must be a good rifleman indeed to hit a running bear. In full flight he looks like a rolling barrel and he travels much faster than you would think him capable. »

BILL GORMAN
« *Today's Maine bear population is estimated at over 23,000. In 2010, 3,062 bears were harvested. Almost all of them were taken over bait or with dogs. It's extremely rare for a hunter to spot and stalk a black bear.*

How to Hunt Moose

The same safety rules, equipment and wearing apparel for deer hunting apply to moose hunting.

At this writing, moose are protected in the State of Maine and in New Brunswick, Nova Scotia and Prince Edward Island, Canada. The other eight provinces have open seasons. «

There are several methods of hunting moose but if you have never been moose hunting I suggest that you employ a guide. It takes much practice

L. L. BEAN
Freeport, Maine
FALL - 1925

BILL GORMAN:
« *My most memorable moose hunt was in Alaska. From about half a mile away, we saw him walk into a low area and he didn't emerge. We crawled on our knees and elbows through snow and water, until, finally, at fifty yards, we saw antlers. At twenty-six yards, we were making moose call after moose call, and all he did was move his head. When he finally stepped up, we were so close that I wished I had a bow instead of a rifle. He was an amazing animal, weighing about 1,600 pounds. He's the one that is over the fireplace in the store in Freeport. If you look closely, you'll see his tines are smashed and there is a hole in the palm of his antler. People think it's from a bullet, but it came from fighting with another moose.*

to call a moose and the average man should not attempt without excellent assistance.

The outdoorsman who uses a camera can enjoy some real sport if he is in a locality where moose are plentiful. Wait until there is snow on the ground, pick out the tracks of a cow moose and her calf, and then slowly trail the animals. If you are careful and the wind is blowing in your face, you stand a good chance of seeing at least one moose. Moose are curious, and will often stand and watch you approach within shooting distance of your camera. »

— CHAPTER 7 —

How to Hunt Ducks and Geese

Present restrictions make duck and goose hunting much more difficult than it was a few years ago when you could use live decoys.

For ducks I recommend a 3 shot 12 gauge Automatic Shot Gun. Use a long range load with number 4 shot.

I use about fourteen removable head decoys. Make your set about 100

~ HOW TO HUNT TURKEY ~

Hunting opportunities for turkeys in Maine are increasing annually, thanks to the efforts of wildlife managers and sportsmen. In just over three decades, Maine's turkey population has gone from near zero to about 60,000 birds, and the birds are found in well over half the state. The heaviest concentrations of turkeys are in southern coastal areas and in Waldo County, where they breed in oak and beech stands and are often seen grazing in grassy pastures with their young. They are especially common around dairy farms because they like the feed corn they can easily find there.

Adult male turkeys are known as "gobblers" or "toms," and juveniles are called "jakes." You can easily identify males, as they are the birds that gobble and have spurs. All males have beards (clusters of hairlike feathers) growing out of the center of their chests, and during courtship, males' heads often display vivid red, white, and blue coloration. Some hens have beards as well, but hunters are discouraged from shooting these older and experienced nesters. The spring hunt is for bearded turkeys only.

You can sit and wait for turkeys in areas where you've seen them before, but the best strategy is mimicking calls to attract lovesick gobblers. The most successful "turkey talk" is the hen yelp. Other useful calls include clucks, cackles, putts, purrs, and aggressive cutting. There is no better way to learn these sounds than to get into the woods and listen to the real thing.

In addition to learning to call, it is a good idea to scout before the season to try to locate as many different turkeys and promising hunting areas as possible.

Also, remember that turkeys have excellent hearing and eyesight — and that they can see color. You'll want to wear complete camouflage and move as little as possible when setting up and calling.

Hunters get a second opportunity at turkeys of either sex in the fall. You are usually hunting either large flocks of hens and their young or bachelor groups of toms. At this time of year the birds are not responding to mating calls, and your strategy should be to scatter a flock and then try to call the birds back together. If you bust up a flock of hens and young birds, the most productive call is the kee-kee, which is basically a high-pitched whistle.

If you take a mature gobbler in the fall, it's a true trophy. Come to think of it, with all of the effort and skill that go into turkey hunting, any bird taken in the spring or fall is one to be proud of.

— *Bill Gorman*

yards off a point of land in an open spot with grass enough around so that you can scull quite close without ducks seeing you. When you see birds coming keep very still until they light in. Lay very low in your gunning float until you are within range. Don't try to kill the whole flock. Pick out the nearest duck and stay with it until it drops before trying for a second bird. Go where wild rice is plentiful if possible and get your decoys out by daylight. The Federal law now allows shooting one-half hour before sunrise to one hour before sunset. »

If you are obliged to hunt where there is no grass or wild rice, construct a blind of boughs, old brush or other natural objects just out of reach of high tide and set your decoys within easy shooting distance. Keep all of your belongings out of sight so that your blind will look natural. Cover your boat with seaweed if possible or beach it where it will not be conspicuous.

BILL GORMAN:
« *The use of live decoys was outlawed in the forties. Hunters would trap a duck and strap a weight to its leg so it couldn't take off. Its calls would attract other ducks. The modern-day version is the battery-operated decoy that flaps its wings or floats tail up, stirring up the water. The battery-operated decoy should be used with a spread of cork decoys.*

Left: A guide, L.T. Patterson, the author's son, Warren Bean and guide with a nice bag of Black Duck shot at Merrymeeting Bay, Maine (left to right).

Right: A good dog comes in handy to retrieve your ducks.

Ducks should be cleaned immediately after they are shot. Remember what the little woman had to say the last time you cleaned a duck in the kitchen sink. Wipe the inside dry and hang by the neck.

Goose hunting is so difficult that you can not expect success without a guide. «

There are two very important things you should attend to before you start hunting either ducks or geese and that is: 1st. Learn to hit a flying target. If there is no trap shooting field where you can go, get an inexpensive hand trap and practice with your duck gun until you can break about 50%. 2nd. Your cap, coat, pants and boots should blend with the duck marsh surroundings. I recommend olive green or khaki.

Unless you learn to hit a flying target you are very apt to stop your gun on a flying duck and shoot way behind it. I have been with good hunters, before live decoys were prohibited, who had good chances all day long without killing a single duck.

(Always keep in mind the safety rules in Chapter 13.)

BILL GORMAN:
» *Today, few hunters would call goose hunting a "guide-only" sport. Canada goose populations have gone from being on the brink of extinction in parts of North America to abundance, thanks to habitat restoration. In some places, their recovery has been almost too successful, leading to complaints about nuisance birds.*

~ DECOYS ~

Handcrafted and realistically painted cork waterfowl decoys are an L.L.Bean tradition that dates back to one morning in 1935 when L.L. grabbed his friend and employee, George Soule, and said, "Let's go duck hunting." After several frustrating hours spent watching black ducks flare away from L.L.'s round-bottom wooden decoys, Soule pronounced them "a mess." L.L. challenged Soule to make something better, and, using insulation cork from a junked refrigeration truck, he did. In fact, Soule's decoys proved so effective at drawing in ducks that 2012 marks the seventy-fifth year that L.L.Bean has included them in its hunting catalog. L.L.Bean cork decoys are made on the same eight-spindle carving machine that George Soule used when, with L.L.'s blessing, he established his own decoy-making shop, first on the second floor of the L.L.Bean factory store and later in a separate building overlooking Casco Bay in Freeport. The machine traces one of Soule's original hardwood masters (dozens of them are still in use), carving eight bird bodies at a time out of Portuguese black cork. The pine heads are carved two per spindle (that is, sixteen at a time) on the same machine. The keel also is pine, the tail is pine plywood, and the eyes are glass. A flat, no-shine paint is sprayed on, and field markings — in the case of black ducks, the blue wing feathers and olive or mustard bill — are painted by hand.

Soule, who died in 1996 at the age of eighty-four, is legendary for his "magnums," larger than life-size black duck decoys that have been used by hunters with uncanny success to draw in the real thing. Soule theorized that the big decoys were simply easier for the ducks to see. They also were realistic in their appearance and, equally important, their movement, a direct result of the cork whose use Soule pioneered. — *Bill Gorman*

— CHAPTER 8 —

How to Hunt Ruffed Grouse

The ruffed grouse, more commonly known as "partridge," is found in every section of the State of Maine. It is probably more abundant and more widely distributed here than anywhere else in the country. The bird is found deep in the big woods and in covers only a short distance from towns and cities.

There are two kinds of grouse in Maine—smart and foolish. The latter are so tame that they can be shot on the ground or on the limbs of trees with a pistol or rifle. These are the birds found in the big woods. They are identical in every way with those found in the settled areas except that they have no fear of humans.

The grouse of the inhabited sections are much smarter than their backwoods brethren. We don't shoot them with rifles or pistols; we don't always hit them with a shotgun. They have been well-termed "the smartest upland game bird that flies."

We Maine hunters look for grouse in farming country. «

We expect to find them in alder and birch thickets, around the edges of fields where berries are plentiful, under wild apple trees, on the oak ridges

BILL GORMAN:
» When early settlers in Maine first cleared forest-lands for farms, grouse in huge numbers were often reported.

This classic Maine Hunting Coat was passed down through three generations of hunters who hunted near Alligator Lake, Maine, before it was donated to the L.L.Bean archives.

in acorn years, even in softwood growths. But we also know we are likely to find them where least expected. There are more than fifty different kinds of food eaten by these birds and finding them is a matter of finding food sources, and, of course, suitable cover.

In the early part of the season we frequently find the birds in flocks of three to six. Later on in the Fall, singles and pairs are more common.

While most hunters prefer to use dogs the birds can be hunted successfully by "walking them" up, as we say. But this requires fast shooting.

Although grouse are more abundant during the first part of the season than the last, many hunters prefer the last two weeks for hunting. That is because the leaves are off the trees and one has a much better chance to see, and hit, these fast-flying birds. They are also likely to be found in more open country, in old apple orchards for example, than during the

Right: Most hunters prefer to use a good dog when hunting Ruffed Grouse.
Opposite: A bird dog is not absolutely necessary when hunting Ruffed Grouse.

early part of October when there are many more kinds of food available.

However, one who plans to hunt grouse in the northern part of the State of Maine will find the birds more plentiful the first part of the season.

One of the best ways to hunt ruffed grouse in the wilderness sections of Maine is to walk slowly along old tote and logging roads. If you flush a grouse and don't get a shot, be on the alert as there probably will be at least one or two additional birds in the vicinity.

Either a .20 gauge or .12 gauge Shotgun will serve your purpose. If you use a double, load one barrel with a No. 7 shell and the other barrel with a No. 6 shell. Use the No. 7 when you shoot at birds nearby, and No. 6 at longer range.

Learn to shoot "on the wing." If you are a fair skeet shooter, you will get your share of the ruffed grouse that you flush, especially where the "territory" is open. Learn to "lead," this knowledge is gained by practice at skeet shooting or using a hand-trap.

When you kill a ruffed grouse, examine the contents of its crop. That will give you an idea as to what the birds are feeding on, and you can then hunt in the vicinity of the places where such food abounds.

Most sportsmen prefer to pluck their game birds, but partridge and woodcock are more easily skinned and taste equally as well. »

BILL GORMAN:
« *It's interesting to note the number of women in these photographs. While the overall number of hunters has declined slightly in recent years, the number of women hunters is growing. More than 16 percent of all hunters in the United States today are women.*

— CHAPTER 9 —

How to Hunt Woodcock

No state in the country offers better woodcock hunting than Maine. The birds are found in all of the coastal counties, in the central section and to some extent in the north. In addition to the thousands of woodcocks that breed and raise families in our birch and alder thickets all of the New

Brunswick and Nova Scotia birds cross Maine on their Fall migration to the southern wintering grounds.

The heaviest concentrations of woodcock are undoubtedly in the expansive covers of Washington County in the eastern part of the state. In the early part of October native birds are found in almost every birch and alder stand. The coastal part of Hancock County also affords excellent shooting. There are many large covers in that section of the state; areas so large that a hunter can spend the better part of a day in one cover.

In the central and western parts of Maine the hunting, for the most part, will be in smaller sections. Lincoln, Knox, Waldo and parts of Kennebec County also afford excellent shooting, mainly in covers that hold from four to a dozen birds at the beginning of the season; more when the flight is underway. Many of these are large enough to accommodate a hunting party of four; others can best be hunted by two men.

The first week of the open season (usually the first of October) may be the surest time to find an abundance of woodcock in Maine. One is sure of finding native birds in the coastal and central sections.

As every veteran woodcock hunter knows it is not possible for us to predict the flight movements; the migrations are guided pretty much by weather conditions. Normally, however, the heavy migration will be about the middle or last of October.

Hunters who have their own dogs and who know woodcock covers when they see them, will have no difficulty in finding good shooting during the Maine season. Since the hunting period is set by Federal authorities it is not possible for me to give the dates in this book. In recent years, however, the period has been in October.

A copy of the Federal migratory bird regulations, issued annually in August, and available from the Fish and Wildlife Service in Washington, D.C., will provide the dates, bag limit, and all other data on the woodcock season.

— CHAPTER 10 —

How to Hunt Pheasants

Maine pheasant hunting is confined to the coastal counties, these birds being unable to withstand deep snow in the northern sections during the winter.

Like grouse, the pheasants are found in the farming sections and around the outskirts of villages. In many cases they frequent the same covers and it is not unusual to find pheasants in woodcock covers.

During the first part of the open season we look for them in fields and covers that contain seed plants or weeds. We also find them in gardens

L. L. Bean Inc.
Fall 1951

from which corn, beans and other foods have been harvested. They also feed on berries and apples but not to the extent that grouse do.

Later, after they have become wise to the ways of men, dogs and guns the birds are more likely to be found in thick cover and in softwoods. A cover so thickly grown with vines and bushes that it is nearly impenetrable will be a favorite hiding place for pheasants.

The State of Maine liberates four to five thousand mature pheasants every spring. These birds breed in the wild and produce flocks ranging from four to a dozen. In addition, the State liberates six to seven thousand nearly grown birds in the latter part of the summer. These supplement the wild stock and are available for hunting in the Fall. Although they are not so plentiful as grouse and woodcock there are enough pheasants in Maine to provide good sport. They are an added reason for late season grouse hunting since the open seasons run together the first two weeks in November.

To any who have not hunted pheasants let me add this warning: The birds are smart, fast-flying, and not easy to kill. Many of the shots will be at ranges over twenty-five yards and in many cases the birds will rise out of gunshot. When wounded they will sometimes elude a top-notch retrieving dog.

It is also possible to combine duck hunting and pheasant hunting in some sections, devoting part of the day to each species. That would be especially true in the coastal areas of Maine where tide is an important factor in hunting waterfowl.

Anyone contemplating hunting pheasants or any other Maine game species should, however, check seasons and regulations in the Maine hunting law handbook, issued annually and obtainable from the Department of Inland Fisheries and Game, Augusta, Maine. «

BILL GORMAN
» *The state of Maine no longer stocks pheasants. They are currently stocked by private gun clubs around the state.*

CHAPTER 11

Hunting Equipment

All modern Rifles not smaller than .25 Calibre are O.K. for deer hunting. I personally use a .25 Calibre Automatic Remington, which carries six shots. Regardless of the kind of gun you buy, do not change too often. Once you get a gun you like, stick to it. You can do much better shooting with a gun with which you are accustomed. »

Although I have used the same rifle for years, I continue to use up all my old shells practicing just before starting on my hunting trip. I want to be sure that the sights are O.K. and that the gun is in perfect working condition. I also buy new shells each season as I have known smokeless powder shells to misfire. Old shells are O.K. for signaling. »

I do not use a regular cartridge belt or clips, instead I carry ten shells in a small zipper leather case that loops onto my belt. Besides the six shells in my rifle, I distribute twelve more in my coat pockets. (28 in all.)

There are many days you will not use a single shell but if you wound a deer you are likely to use quite a few and he may take you so far from camp that you will need many more for signaling. (See page 45.)

BILL GORMAN
« The L.L.Bean retail store didn't formally sell firearms until 1984. But in the early days, L.L. would often purchase a gun, determine it didn't suit his purposes (for whatever reason), and he'd put it out on the floor to sell it.

BILL GORMAN
« L.L. was able to confidently stand behind everything he sold because he personally used all that gear. That philosophy still stands. All our hunting and fishing employees spend many days in the field and on the water. Personally, I'm in the woods thirty weeks a year.

Left: Always make sure that your sights are O.K. and that your rifle is in perfect working condition before starting on your hunting trip.

– BOWHUNTING –

If you're new to the sport of archery, you may want to consider starting with a compound bow. Because they use cams or elliptical wheels to reduce the force necessary to hold the bows at full draw, compound bows are remarkably consistent and accurate, allowing you to become competent very quickly. With a little practice, you'll find yourself routinely making forty-yard shots.

Once you're proficient with the compound bow, you may desire a greater challenge. That is the time to give a traditional wood recurve, longbow, or flatbow a try. Many archery enthusiasts prefer the challenge of the old stick and string and even build their own wooden bows and arrows.

The range of archery equipment is vast, and advances are being made all the time. Bows come in a variety of lengths and are made from wood, fiberglass and graphite, or carbon composites. Arrows may be wooden shafts with feather fletchings or aluminum, carbon fiber, or composite materials fletched with plastic vanes. In the past, tips were broadheads made of steel or stone; today's tips often sport surgically sharpened razorblades — some fixed in position, others set within the broadheads and deploying on contact.

Add to that mechanical string releases, stabilizers, lighted bowsights, detachable quivers, and more, and you have some very sophisticated equipment.

Whether you choose to use modern or primitive equipment, bowhunting is an extra excuse to spend time in the woods and a thrilling way to harvest an animal. — *Bill Gorman*

I carry two compasses. (See Chapter 15 "How to Use a Compass.")

For other small equipment I carry about twenty matches in a small sealed container for emergency use only. Also other matches for daily use. One medium size pocket knife, one sheath knife or small belt axe, a vest pocket flashlight, a few strips of celluloid or small fire kindler and a small pocket waterproof game bag in which I carry a lunch. Also, drag line about 8 ft. of strong window cord is good for hanging up and dragging out deer.

If you do not have a guide make your equipment just as light as possible. If you do have a guide See Chapter 38.

If you are going to camp and do your own cooking, you will find grub lists in Chapter 33. I suggest that you choose food that is easy to prepare, especially so if you can go to the door of your camp with an auto.

If your party is more than two or you plan to stay more than six days you will need to increase the amount proportionately.

Non-residents in Maine can not camp and kindle fires from May 1 to December 1 in the open without a registered guide for every five members of your party, except at public camp sites. A copy of either the Game Laws or Fishing Laws may be obtained by writing the Fish and Game Commissioner, Augusta, Maine. »

BILL GORMAN
« *L.L. makes no mention of bow hunting, but he was interested in it. One often-told story is of the day in the fifties that a Bear Archery representative visited and set up a target in a back storeroom of the store on Main Street. L.L. told his friend and employee Wid Griffin, "Give it a whirl!" Wid shot an arrow right out the window into downtown Freeport.*

"Corrosion is the worst enemy of firearms," read the catalog copy for Bean's Gun Grease back in 1948. A four-ounce tube sold for just fifty cents post paid.

CHAPTER 12

Wearing Apparel

As I have been quite a successful deer hunter for the past thirty-one years (shooting 32 deer) I am taking the liberty of recommending just what I wear.

Shoes: One pair 12" Leather Top Rubbers. I also take along a pair of 6 ½" Moccasins to wear dry days on the ridges before snow comes.

Stockings: Two pairs knee-length heavy woolen and two pairs light woolen.

Underwear: Two union suits same as worn at home. «

Pants: One pair medium weight all wool with knit or zipper bottom. Also wear from home your heaviest business suit.

Coat: One medium weight, brilliant scarlet with game pocket in back.

Shirt: Two medium weight, all wool; one to be red in case you go out to drag in deer without coat.

Cap: Lightweight scarlet with earlaps that can be worn up or down.

Gloves: One pair lightweight red woolen or red cotton.

Handkerchiefs: Six red bandanas. Do not use white in woods. I also recommend colored toilet paper.

Miscellaneous: One pair heavy Suspenders, one heavy Belt, one very light weight Sweater or Wind Breaker, one Silk Rain Shirt, one Pajama Suit, two Towels, a few Toilet Articles, and one pair Slippers. Coming from a long hunt change to slippers and light stockings. This is important to keep feet in best condition. «

For deer hunting I believe it is very important to wear scarlet coat and cap, but if you don't care to go to the expense, buy a cheap Coldfire rayon red vest to wear over your coat to avoid accidental shooting.

Some old hunters do not wear red because they believe that it frightens deer. This is a mistaken idea.

BILL GORMAN

» *L.L. Bean still sells union suits, but most people buy them for campwear. As a base layer, merino wool is superior to cotton in cold, damp weather.*

BILL GORMAN

» *L.L. would have embraced today's high-performance gear. He never shied away from innovation. He introduced the Maine Hunting Shoe in 1912, after all, and it was the best footwear available at the time: rubber bottom, leather upper, and a snow seal. It kept your feet warm and dry.*

Originally sold to customers in 1912, L.L. Bean came up with the idea for the Maine Hunting Shoe when he returned from a hunting trip with cold, wet feet.

This red plaid hunting coat was given to grandson Leon Gorman by L.L. Bean's second wife, Claire, in the early 1970s. It is the last deer-hunting coat L.L. used.

I have always worn red and have proof that it does not frighten deer. Do not take unnecessary chances with your life.

These recommendations apply only where car or boat takes you to camp door. If camp is located where you are obliged to walk or canoe quite a distance, I recommend that you wear hunting clothes from home. Also eliminate some other articles that you feel you can get along without.

— ADVANCES IN OUTDOOR APPAREL —

Thanks to advances in fabrics, today's hunter is much more comfortable than those in L.L.'s day. That translates into greater success because the longer you can sit still and quiet, the more successful you'll be. Here are my suggestions for today's hunter:

Shoes: Two pairs, one insulated, one not. I like the Maine Hunting Shoe when I bow hunt because it gives me tactile feedback. Tall rubber boots are also good. The taller the boot, the better it conceals your scent.

Socks: Heavy wool socks, wool hiking socks, or synthetic-wool blend socks. I wear one of these or a combination, depending on where I am. They insulate and wick away moisture, so my feet stay comfortable.

Underwear: Merino wool base layer. Merino wool is super comfortable, wicks moisture, and doesn't carry scent. If it's early archery season, I won't wear a base layer.

Pants: Pants made from a light, breathable synthetic material. Northweave is rugged, and it won't hold moisture like cotton will; it's as close as you can get without being actual cotton. If it's extremely cold, I wear my wool hunting pants with a waterproof/breathable membrane to block the wind.

Shirt: L.L. Bean Northweave synthetic shirt. Depending on the season, I may add a sweater, a light synthetic vest, and a windproof layer on top.

Cap and Vest: Blaze orange. You may also want a wool cap and a windproof balaclava.

Miscellaneous: Comfortable slippers. The first thing you want to do when you come into a lodge is take off your boots and put on your slippers so you don't track the outdoors inside.

— *Bill Gorman*

— CHAPTER 13 —

Safety Rules

During the 1953 hunting season there were 7 fatal and 25 nonfatal hunting accidents in Maine. Of the 32 persons shot, 12 were mistaken for game. »

Never have a loaded gun in camp. Load and unload your gun outside with muzzle pointing away from camp. Leave your rifle in camp with the chamber open.

Never point your gun, loaded or unloaded, in the general direction of another person.

Do not shoot anything until you are positive it is not a person. *Always* keep your safety on when in company with another hunter. »

Never pull the trigger just for fun.

Never shoot at bottles or other hard surfaces from which a bullet may glance.

Always look to see if a gun is empty before handling it.

Always break down a gun before climbing through fence. (See following page.)

Never carry a loaded gun in a car. In many states, including the State of Maine, it is unlawful.

Never pull a gun, by the muzzle, from a boat or automobile.

Wear Scarlet Coat and Cap.

Every big game hunter should know how to *build a fire* in a rain or snow storm. A hunter, with plenty of matches, froze to death in a snow storm near one of my camps through the fact that he was unable to build a fire.

Personally I always carry a few ounces of fire kindler and when out in a bad storm occasionally build a fire for practice as follows:

1st. Gather plenty of dead, sound branches from black growth trees (pine is preferable) and plenty of bark from white birch trees when handy.

2nd. Scrape the snow off an open spot on high ground and brush it clean with fir boughs.

BILL GORMAN
« *Hunting is a far safer sport today, thanks to hunter safety courses and blaze orange apparel. In 2010, there were no hunting-related fatalities and only seven injuries in Maine.*

BILL GORMAN
« *Some states have minimum antler sizes for animals that can be harvested. I like minimums because they increase hunter safety. They force people to be more aware of what they're shooting at and they promote larger animal growth.*

— HUNTER SAFETY —

In L.L.'s time, hunting was not the safest sport in Maine. Back in the days when success could mean the difference between eating and going hungry, some hunters were less discriminating about identifying targets. It was not surprising to read that a hunter had been "mistaken for game" and wounded or killed.

These days hunting accidents in Maine are much less frequent, thanks to education, regulations, and precautions that hunters take to protect themselves.

Applicants for adult hunting licenses now must show proof of having held an adult hunting license since 1976 or of having completed an approved hunter safety course. These requirements ensure that hunters have been taught how to properly use a firearm, hunter ethics and responsibilities, and survival and first aid. Additional training in the use of map and compass is a precaution against hunters getting lost in the woods.

Anyone hunting for deer or moose during the firearms season in most states must wear hunter orange. The specific articles of clothing and the amount of orange they contain differ by state and season, but obviously wearing fluorescent orange increases hunters' visibility. (The only hunters not affected by this are waterfowlers hunting from boats or blinds or with decoys, as they are typically removed from traditional big-game hunting areas.) This regulation has had a significant affect on reducing hunting accidents.

By its nature, with hunters being dressed in full camouflage and using decoys and calls to lure turkeys to their position, turkey hunting has the potential to be dangerous. The state has put together a "Spring Wild Turkey Hunter's Guide," which emphasizes the importance of bird identification, ethics, and safety. Some of the tips given are:

Never wear the colors red, white, or blue, as these are the colors of a gobbler's head and are used by hunters to differentiate between a gobbler and a hen.

Always select a calling position that provides a backdrop at least as wide as your shoulders (shielding your back).

Always be able to see at least forty yards in a 180-degree field of view in order to spot approaching hunters.

Always consider that sounds you hear may be being made by another hunter.

If you see another hunter approaching, make your *presence* known by waving, shining a light, or by voice signal.

Never try to stalk a turkey, as this may lead you to another hunter.

Be *careful* to cover up your bird when transferring it out of the woods — preferably by wrapping it in an orange carry bag. This will prevent other hunters for mistaking you for a bird.

Thanks to these and other efforts to make hunters aware of potential dangers, pursuing game is now a much safer pastime. — *Bill Gorman*

3rd. Lay down any paper you have, fire kindler and small strips of bark.

4th. Add very small dead, sound limbs and a few pine whittlings.

5th. Light the fire kindler and add small pieces of limbs as fast as the flames will take them.

6th. Keep adding small wood until coals begin to form. You now have a fire that will take large, sound, deadwood even if it is quite wet.

— CHAPTER 14 —

Signals for Hunters

It is very important that you have a system of signals that every member of your party will recognize. I recommend the following: When you want to get in touch with another member fire two shots about five seconds apart. Anyone of your party hearing it will reply with two shots. You answer with one shot. He immediately starts looking for you. After traveling ten minutes he will fire one shot and you will answer with one. When he believes he is near you, he will "Hello." Not receiving an answer

Left: Hunting mishaps account for about one-third of the nation's accidental gun fatalities. Gun barrels should be checked for foreign objects before firing.

Middle: When crossing a fence, gun should be broken and set on other side before hunter climbs over. Most hunting mishaps result from an accidental firing of hunter's own gun.

Right: Guns should never be used as a prop or "crutch" by hunters. Improper handling of firearms accounts for a substantial portion of all fatal U.S. hunting accidents.

he will fire one more shot which you will answer with one. Continue this one shot which you will answer with one. Continue this one shot conversation until you are within hailing distance. After calling for help and receiving a reply *do not* leave your position.

CHAPTER 15

How to Use a Compass

There is no excuse for getting lost if you carry a good compass and know how to use it.

Camping places are invariably located on trail, tote road, stream, lake, telephone wire, etc. We will say that your camp is on a good sized stream or well defined road running North and South. You cross the stream or road and hunt to the East for several hours. When you want to go to camp all you need to do is travel West. Hold compass so needle arrow points to "N" then pick out some object in a due West direction and go to it. Keep repeating this and you are sure to hit your road but it may be a mile or more below or above your camp. You are out of the woods anyway and if you have been over the road a few times you will soon see landmarks that will tell you which way to go.

Lakes, old railroads, telephone wires, etc., always run in some general direction and you must be sure of this direction when you start out and always be sure which side you are hunting on.

Before starting out I usually get someone in the party to help make a rough sketch of the territory and always carry it with me. A rough

L.L. Bean felt the dials of most compasses were too "cluttered up with figures, lines, and ornaments." So he created this plain dial for ease of use "even on a very dark day."

— HOW TO USE A GPS —

The modern tool for navigating the outdoors is the Global Positioning System (GPS) receiver. Besides providing your exact position on the earth, a handheld GPS will guide you to your destination, give you information to keep you on course and tell you how far you have to go. It lays electronic breadcrumbs called "waypoints" so you can retrace your route, even on the sort of spontaneous side trip that might cause a lesser-equipped hunter to lose his way.

At first, only the military used GPS, but quality mapping devices can now be had for about the cost of a riflescope or good tent. Of course, technology will continue to improve at a fast clip, and both features and prices are sure to change.

While sophisticated, the technology is not difficult to master. The GPS searches the sky for satellite signals. When the GPS finds at least two signals, it establishes your current latitude and longitude and displays your location on a digital map on the screen.

Today's units are so powerful it is no longer necessary to stand in a clearing to get a signal; a clear view of the sky is sufficient. To get the best results, remember to stop and lock into a signal before you head into the trees. If you are wearing a backpack, fix the GPS to the shoulder strap so it is pointed at the sky. If you carry the unit in your hand, avoid swinging your arms because the movement can confuse the receiver.

If you own a GPS, you may be tempted to throw away your paper map and compass. Don't give in to that temptation. Batteries can die. Heavy tree cover and steep and narrow valleys can interfere with satellite signals. And if you drop your GPS in a stream, it may cease to function altogether. The best piece of gear that you take into the woods is the one between your ears. No piece of technology replaces a working knowledge of traditional navigational skills. — *Bill Gorman*

map of this kind is a big help to find the very shortest way to camp.

At times you will feel sure your compass is wrong. The best way to overcome this feeling is to carry two compasses. In checking one compass against the other, place them eight to ten feet apart and away from your gun or other metal. Another reason for carrying two compasses is that one might get broken. In fact, compasses have been known to get out of order. When compass needle swings back and forth several times and finally settles in the same direction on two or three tests, it is O.K.

CHAPTER 16

How to Find a Lost Hunter

In case one of your party does not show up at camp when night falls as has previously been his custom, do not get excited and do not do a thing until 6:00 P.M. If you start signaling before 6:00 P.M. other hunters who have not gotten into camp are likely to butt in and make it very misleading.

Eat your supper and see that the lantern is full of oil. Then go outside with rifle, lantern and flashlight. At exactly 6:00 P.M. fire two shots. Listen a moment for a reply. Not hearing any, walk about one-quarter mile and repeat your signal. If you get a reply, see a fire or note any odor of smoke, continue the signals, always walking in the general direction that you believe your man is located.

In the meantime what is the "lost" hunter to do? If, in late afternoon, he realizes that he is lost or so far from camp that he can not get in, he selects a sheltered spot where dry wood is handy, starts a fire and collects a lot of wood before dark. At exactly 6:00 P.M. he listens for a signal. On hearing it, he answers and the signals continue the same as in the daytime. Hearing no signal he wastes none of his shells but pounds a signal at regular intervals with a club on a sound dead tree. If there is no dead tree available, select a live tree and peel off a spot of bark where he wants to pound.

In the morning, if not sure of the direction to camp, he is not to leave the spot or shoot except to answer his party's signals. Keep smoke going and pound out a few signals about every ten minutes.

The party at camp should not stay out too late. Notify a Game Warden or Sheriff during the night and continue the search at daybreak.

By following these simple rules the lost hunter or his party have nothing to worry about.

(It is a good idea to mark all trails a short distance each side of camp. Lay down small limbs of black growth with broken end pointing toward camp. Your party can do it in less than an hour.) «

BILL GORMAN
» *Posted in one of his hunting camps, L.L. had a list of rules. Rule number 7 was: "If you get lost, come straight back to camp."*

CHAPTER 17

How to Fish for Salmon, Trout and Togue

Of all the fresh water game fishing, Salmon is my favorite. They hit hard, jump high and fight every inch of that way to the net.

During the first month after the ice goes out in the Spring I find trolling with bait the most successful. I use a sewed-on Smelt on one rod and Night Crawlers on the other. I recommend a 7 ½ ounce 9 ½ ft. Trolling Rod, level winding 100 yard Reel, 25 lb. test Nylon Line with markings at 50, 75 and 100 ft., a 15" Leader, two Swivels and a 12" Snelled 2/0 Hook. Row slowly and run from 50 to 100 feet of Line until you land your first fish. Note how

Below: Fishing party with Salmon and Trout caught at Moosehead Lake 1939. Over half of these fish were taken on Live Bait Fly as described on page 50. Left to right: Dr. A.L. Gould, Willis Libby, Levi Patterson, and L.L. Bean.

BILL GORMAN

» *Not everyone knows what a gut snell is. The short section of line in front of the hook would have been silkworm gut, a natural material, so it had to be soaked before use to make it pliable. Longer leaders would have been made from catgut. Now, of course, we have monofilament and other synthetic materials for lines and leaders.*

much line you had out and continue using the same length.

For sewing on smelts and shiners I recommend the following method: Place a few gut hooks in a can of water or minnow bucket so snell will be pliable when ready to bait up. «

1st. String minnow lengthways on snell by passing hook through mouth,

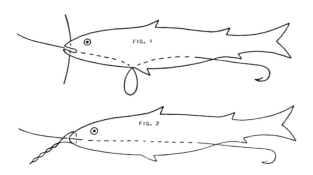

out at belly then right back through same hole and out at side as shown in Fig. 1.

2nd. Draw snell tight which takes out loop and forces snell to pass straight through minnow as shown in Fig. 2.

3rd. Stick point of hook into side of minnow between the two tail fins.

4th. Close mouth with little wire as shown in Figs. 1 and 2.

5th. Crowd minnow back into hook so as to form a bend.

6th. Wind twisted wire around snell twice and try trolling at side of boat. Bait should turn to imitate wounded minnow. If too slow put in more bend. When satisfactory, wind balance of wire around snell and you are ready to fish.

The little wires cost only 15c for a tube of fifty.

When you have no luck trolling, try changing your bait to different levels in the water by adding to, or reducing, the weight of your sinkers.

After the first month I run a live bait fly, as illustrated (right), on one rod and a sewed-on minnow on the other. A shiner hooked through the lips as shown will keep alive for about two hours. Do not stick tail hook into minnow. I use a 5 ½ ounce Fly Rod for the live bait fly. Later in the season when it gets warm and the fish go into deep water it is much more

Introduced in 1951, this new leader pack "does away with fussing with loose coils."

difficult to get them to take surface bait. Many times it becomes a question of going home empty handed or resorting to a somewhat unsportsmanlike method of deep trolling.

For deep trolling you need a very stiff rod, a solid 150 yard reel and metal covered 100 yard line. Use a set of spoons size 2 to 6/0 according to the depth of water with plenty of swivels. Run sewed-on minnow on one rod and night crawlers on the other. Use a short snelled 2/0 hook without leader so that bait is not over 8 inches from tail spoon. Keep a few hooks soaking in bait pail as it is about impossible to sew on minnows with a dry snelled hook.

Always carry a ruler of some kind to be sure fish is legal length. When returning fish to water wet both hands and use a hook disgorger.

Trout and togue are caught in the same way as salmon except you troll

⁓ CATCH AND RELEASE ⁓

L. L. Bean, Inc.
Spring 1971

What we consider unsportsmanlike has always been a shifting matter of opinion and perspective. This has never been more true than in the conservation ethics of practicing catch and release, which has become a big force in modern angling and fishing in Maine.

The idea of releasing fish unharmed — to protect their numbers and the quality of the fishing experience for everyone — began in the late fifties in some of the country's best-known trout-fishing regions. Catch and release has become a tremendously successful sport fisheries management practice, taking hold especially with the rise in popularity of fly-fishing in the past twenty years. Many anglers release every fish they catch, or plan to harvest only a few for the frying pan over the course of a fishing season, and the state has made many of our best waters catch and release by regulation to protect trout and salmon numbers and angling quality. Often combined with restrictions for artificial lures only or fly-fishing only, catch and release is an important part of Maine's conservation landscape.

That said, I'm not one to condemn someone for occasionally keeping fish, because I'm going to. It's part of fishing — it's part of our heritage. You should be proud to eat what you harvest, and there shouldn't be any apologies for that. Of course, there are exceptions. For instance, I won't kill a species of fish that is on a downward population trend. Catch and release is a great way that we can enjoy the outdoors and reduce our impact in places as part of our resource management. That's what conservation is: It's the responsible use of a renewable resource. — *Bill Gorman*

Opposite: The catalog copy for Bean's Angle Worm Food explained that "fish will take a lively worm when they will not notice one that is half dead."

a little slower and fish a little nearer shore for trout and farther away for togue.

Do not strike your fish too quickly. Strip off a few yards of line so as to give it time to get bait and hook well into its mouth. This is important and applies to both trout and salmon, the former especially are very slow taking in bait.

I have recommended a metal covered line which I prefer but any line which tests thirty-six pounds or more is O.K. Fly fishing is explained in Chapters 22, 23, 24 & 25. All game fish should be cleaned immediately after they are caught.

How to Care for Minnows and Worms

Minnows and worms for bait need to be kept fresh and lively. For minnows on short trips I recommend a puckering string, canvas bucket with an inside wire cage. On warm days place a piece of ice on top of cage under puckering string. On cool days or after ice has melted, dip bucket in water often enough to keep canvas damp. Water should be changed about every hour. When in camp remove cage and submerge in cold water.

On long trips I recommend a large bait pail with removable inside cage. Place a piece of ice on top of pail in such a way that the steady *drip-drip-drip* from it into the pail will supply an artificial means of injecting oxygen into the water and keeping it cool. On arrival at your destination remove cage and submerge in cold water.

Angle worms and night crawlers should be packed in moss in a good size container. Get an eight quart galvanized pail, put in a large piece of ice and place container of worms on top. Then cover pail

with old piece of damp cloth. Renew ice as needed. When bait fishing, I see to it that my minnows and worms have very careful attention.

There are two kinds of garden angle worms, light and dark. The dark worms are much better as they keep fresh and lively much longer than the light worms.

Night crawlers and angle worms can be kept all winter in a wooden box filled with damp moss, in the cellar.

A little oatmeal, coffee grounds or cornmeal makes good food. Feed them every two weeks. (Regular worm food is now available in small cans.)

Sitting and wishing won't change your fate- The Lord provides the fishing but, you have to dig the bait. »

BILL GORMAN
« *Live bait is still widely used, but today's anglers also have a choice of synthetic flies, worms, and frogs. L.L. Bean carries only biodegradable plastic lures, so you don't have to worry about lost lures being consumed by fish and endangering wildlife.*

CHAPTER 19

How to Fish for White Perch

Use a bait casting rod. A Number 1 hook will be O.K. Angle worms are all right for bait. If you use a float, adjust it so that the hook will be about three or four inches from the bottom of the lake.

If you fish without a float, use a small sinker, pinching it to the line six or eight inches above the hook. Let the bait sink slowly. When the sinker hits bottom, raise it nine or ten inches and keep it there for a couple of minutes. Raise it slowly and make another cast.

If you are fishing on a lake where white perch are known to be plentiful, and you don't have any luck, paddle your canoe or row your boat to another section of the lake and make several casts. If this isn't successful, try another and still another spot. When you do catch a white perch, stay in the vicinity because they are "school" fish and you may catch a dozen or more as fast as you can lower and raise your baited hook.

Just at dark is the best time to fish. At certain seasons they will take a fly at this time of day. Use your regular fly rod and wet trout flies, as shown on page 68, with a little lead "twiston" on your leader. Let fly sink well under water and retrieve it slowly.

When they are taking a fly you will get them faster and have a lot more sport than with bait.

If there is an old log dam at the outlet of the lake or pond you are fishing, try your luck in the deep-hole just below the dam. It is a good place to fish at the opening of the season. «

BILL GORMAN
» *White perch were valuable fish to early settlers in Maine. Because of this they were introduced into many waters where they were not native. Today, as in L.L.'s time, they are abundant.*

Right: L.L. Bean's well-stocked private trout pond in Freeport, Maine, where fly rods, reels, lines, leaders and flies are tried out.

L. L. Bean, Inc.
Spring 1963

— CHAPTER 20 —

How to Fish for Black Bass

Pound for pound, Black Bass are the gamest fish in Maine. »

The season opens late. In Maine, bass can not be taken with bait before June 21st. However, three per day may be taken with fly from June 1st to June 20th. If you have never done fly fishing for bass you have missed a lot of fun.

During the first of the open season (June 1st to July 10th) I use flies. Later when the water gets warm, bass feed on or near the bottom and will

This trolling reel was the personal property of L.L. Bean. It is model No. 67 - Long Beach.

BILL GORMAN

» Bass are found in 613 lakes and ponds in all sixteen of the state's counties and in several of our large rivers, comprising more than five hundred thousand acres of waters in all. Regulations have evolved to sustain bass fishing while allowing more access to this great family sport. And the tackle has evolved dramatically, allowing the kid with a worm and bobber, the bait fisherman, and the fly-fishing purist to all pursue bass as they like.

notice bottom activities more quickly than disturbances on the surface.

Live minnows and frogs are excellent bait for bass fishing. A minnow three inches long is large enough. If you use frogs, choose the small ones. Hook minnows and frogs through both upper and lower lips, pointing hook upward under lower jaw. Start fishing immediately after hook is properly set.

For equipment a rod of medium stiffness, 9 feet long will prove satisfactory. Line should be of 15 lbs. test. Sinkers should weigh about one ounce.

If worms are used, those that are clean and bright will prove most satisfactory. Use a No. 1 or No. 2 hook with gut snell. Put the worm on corkscrew fashion so that about half an inch of worm projects below the point of the hook. When completed, no part of the hook should show.

You can often get a bass to take artificial bait by trolling with colored minnow or a red and white plug.

A very enjoyable day may be had by making up a picnic party. Your Guide will take along everything necessary for a bass chowder. All you have to do is catch bass and meet at the prearranged camp site. Bass makes the best chowder of any fish that swims. «

— CHAPTER 21 —

How to Fish for Small Brook Trout

This is an inexpensive sport enjoyed by a large number of fishermen right near their own homes. It is practically all bait fishing. Angle worms are about the only bait used in Maine.

I recommend a 9 foot telescope steel rod, an inexpensive level winding reel, a 25 yard, hard surfaced line, an eight-inch snelled No. 2 hook and a fairly large sinker.

Most trout brooks are very bushy and many times you will find trout in the most difficult places to fish.

This is where your telescope rod comes in. By telescoping it up to four or five feet it makes it easier getting through the bushes and into the hole you want to fish.

Do not use a small, soft line, as it snarls so easily you will spend most of your time unsnarling it from brush and bushes. An old level fly line makes an excellent line for brook trout fishing. »

When fishing in a still pool do not yank too suddenly. Give the fish time to get bait well into its mouth.

I carry my worms packed in moss in a bait pocket in my coat. On warm days I occasionally dampen them with cold water. Take plenty of worms so that you may change bait often as trout will take a wiggly worm when they will not take a dead one.

Place a few leaves or moss in the bottom of your creel before putting in your first trout and continue to do so with each trout you catch.

When convenient, clean trout in the stream before placing them in your basket. They keep better and clean easier when first caught.

When bait fishing for small trout on a pond with boat or raft, let the bait sink slowly until sinker hits bottom. Then raise about a foot. Hold it there for one or two minutes before making another cast. Do not yank too quickly. Once you have located fish do not leave the spot until you are sure they have stopped biting. »

BILL GORMAN
« Worms will always catch trout, no question about it. But these days you can also have a lot of fun, and catch a lot of fish, using a medium-action fly rod designed for 2-to-4 weight lines. A shorter rod (less than eight feet) is easier to manage in dense cover, but a longer rod allows you to do some high-sticking if you want to drift a nymph through a plunge pool.

BILL GORMAN
« Maine has been famous for brook trout fishing since well before this book was written — and rightfully so. No other experience conjures the Maine outdoors better than catching brook trout. In fact, Maine has more native brook trout habitat and the largest population of native and wild brook trout in the United States. And while the landlocked salmon is the state's "official" fish, the brook trout was also recognized as one of Maine's heritage fish in 2005.

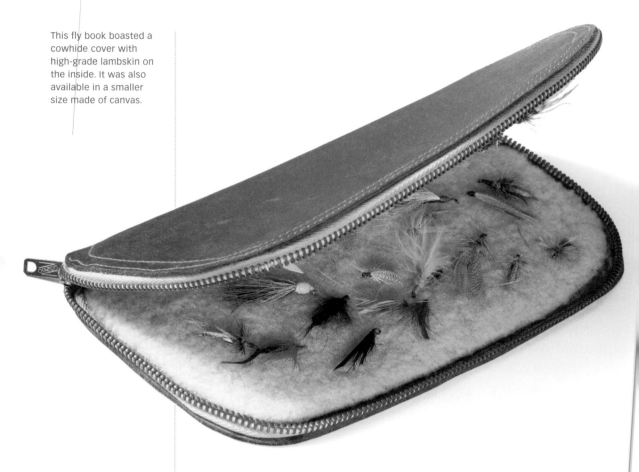

This fly book boasted a cowhide cover with high-grade lambskin on the inside. It was also available in a smaller size made of canvas.

CHAPTER 22

Fly Fishing – General

You may have read or have heard that fly fishing is an art that requires expensive equipment and the mastery of many difficult tricks. Perhaps you have neglected this part of fishing because you have considered the sport hard to learn. But you certainly won't learn to fly fish if you don't try. The more casts you make the better you will understand the technique. Don't attempt at first to make casts of 60 or 70 feet like many experienced fly fishermen do. Most fish are taken within 35 or 40 feet of the angler.

Although dry fly fishing is faster than wet fly fishing, you can use dry flies to advantage only at certain periods of the year. For early fishing in the Spring you probably will depend on bait fishing. Then comes the wet flies and later, dry flies. (Regardless of the lure you use during the early part of the season, or the variety of wet or dry fly that you employ later on, you will get a strike occasionally, that is only natural.)

There are often times when both occupants of a canoe can fish successfully, but as a rule there should be but one person fly fishing from a canoe. After you have enjoyed an hour's sport, change seats with your companion and let him fish.

If you are on a lake that you are not familiar with, let your companion paddle slowly parallel to and about 100 feet from the shore. Fish to right and left. If you don't get a strike, try again about 200 feet from shore. For bass and pickerel, make your casts as near the shore as possible among the water plants. »

When you use a wet fly, allow plenty of time after you make a cast so that the fly will have a chance to sink several feet. Retrieve it slowly so that the fly will be agitated.

If it is the right season for dry fly fishing, I suggest that you paddle along slowly until you see a fish rise to the surface for food. Then start fly fishing. If you are fishing with wet flies and see a fish leap to the surface, change to a dry fly and try your luck in the vicinity of the action which you have witnessed. Always use leaders that are well soaked and pliable.

Whatever type of rod, reel and line that you use, it is a good idea to use heavy line with a heavy rod, and a light-weight line with a light-weight rod. (See chart on Page 64). Don't make the mistake of using your fly rod as a derrick to lift a caught fish into the canoe, because nets are made for that purpose.

There are many and varied artificial attractions for wet and dry fly fishing. It is well to take along a practical assortment of flies in your tackle box, as well as several leaders of various lengths.

BILL GORMAN
« *L.L. Bean took a leadership role in environmental stewardship when we stopped manufacturing and carrying felt-soled wading shoes. Felt-soled footgear is a problem because it transports algae like didymo (rock snot), whirling disease, and other invasive organisms from stream to stream. Several states have now banned felt-soled shoes, and most wading shoe manufacturers are moving away from them.*

Below: Follow directions in our book and this will not happen.

L.L.BEAN
Manufacturer
FREEPORT MAINE

Copyright 1930 by L. L. Bean

SPRING CATALOG 1930

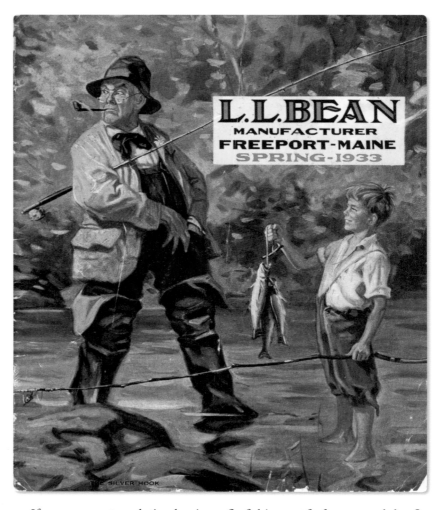

THE SILVER HOOK

L.L.BEAN
MANUFACTURER
FREEPORT-MAINE
SPRING-1933

If you are contemplating buying a fly fishing outfit for wet and dry fly fishing, the first thing to be considered is the rod. If for wet fly fishing get a medium action. If for dry fly fishing a stiff action. If for both wet and dry a medium stiff action. Personally I do not care for a soft action rod for any kind of fishing. A rod 8 ½ or 8 feet in length is about right. If it is 8 ½ feet long it should weigh approximately five ounces if constructed of split bamboo.

The next thing to buy is a reel. I like a single action reel with a capacity of about 50 yards of line.

A good fly line is essential. As most of your casts on trout streams will average less than 40 feet, it is necessary to have a line more than 25 yards in length. You may prefer a tapered line, perhaps a level line. I prefer a Bug Taper Line for all kinds of fly fishing. This is a matter of personal choice, and after a few seasons of trout fishing you will find that you are constantly experimenting in lines, reels, flies and other equipment.

You will also need a tube or bottle of fly dope to keep the midges and mosquitoes away and a pocket knife, with hook hone set in handle, also hole in bolster for shaping hooks.

— CHAPTER 23 —

Fly Casting

Actually there is no such thing as fly casting. It's the line that's cast and not the fly. The fly simply rides along as a passenger. Keep this in mind and you will soon learn how to cast. In bait casting the lure carries out the line but in fly casting the line carries out the lure. »

The caster in Fig. 1 is ready to begin; Right foot forward, right thumb parallel on the handle; left hand grasping the line which lays out about thirty feet in front on the water.

Starting the back cast, the left hand is brought slightly back to straighten out the line and at the same time lift the rod slowly to the 10:00 A.M. position and without hesitation, "snap" the rod back to the 2:00 P.M. position still grasping the line in the left hand which now travels slightly up. The line has now left the water and is flying back in a wide arc. Give it time to go back straight as shown in Fig. 2.

The rod has now reached the 2:00 P.M. position in Fig. 2 and the line is parallel to the water. The forward cast is started by "snapping" the rod for-

BILL GORMAN
« *L.L.'s point about casting the line, with the fly along as the passenger, is a well-known one. But I love the quote, "Actually there is no such thing as fly casting." It captures L.L.'s straightforward style perfectly.*

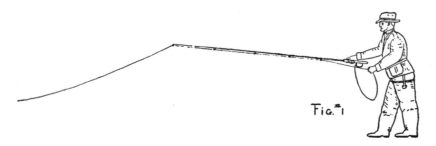

Fig. 1

Right: All the quick action of your rod is between 10 and 2 o'clock. Never let it go back beyond 2 o'clock.

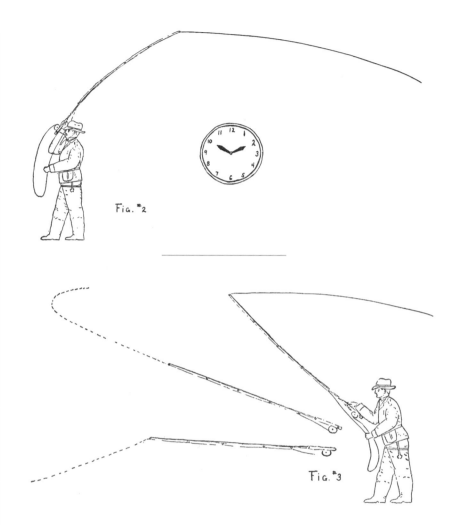

Fig. #2

Fig. #3

ward to the 10:00 A.M. position and releasing the line from the left hand at this point. The fly will strike the water in front of the leader and your cast should produce results.

Properly executed the cast should follow the pattern shown in Fig. 3 and that's all there is to fly casting. From here on perfection depends on practice.

Common Faults Of The Beginner

Fault No. 1 - Trying to pick up a crooked line from the water. No perfect cast can be made unless the line is straight at the start.

Fault No. 2 - Starting the "snap back" at the 8:00 A.M. position instead of the 10:00 A.M. position.

Fault No. 3 - Not giving the line time to straighten out on the back cast. This is a difficult fault to correct. Try changing your position by putting the left foot forward so you can swing around and watch the line straighten out behind you. After a little practice you will notice a slight pull as the line straightens out.

Fault No. 4 - Bringing the rod back beyond 2:00 P.M. position. This causes the spring to leave the rod, and the line, when started, will pile up. Try to imagine you are going to throw a potato from the tip of your rod.

Fault No. 5 - Releasing the line from the left hand position before the rod reaches the 10:00 A.M. position. This also causes the line to pile up.

Fault No. 6 - Trying to cast too much line. The longer the cast, the more difficult it is. Fish are caught at from thirty to forty feet in stream fishing. No need for a long cast here.

Fault No. 7 - Casting "stiff arm." Every advantage should be taken of the leverage in the forearm and wrist. This leverage can only be had when the elbow is near the body. One well known instructor recommends placing a bottle of "Scotch" under the right arm during practice.

Fault No. 8 - Lunging and thrashing. Remember your line, leader and fly only weighs a few ounces and no brute strength is necessary to throw this weight. Fly casting is a sport that requires rhythmic coordination between mind and body. It can only come through practice and patience. It is difficult to see your own faults, so it might help if you had a friend read these instructions, then coach you. »

———————————

No fly rod, no matter how expensive, will perform well unless the fly line is properly fitted to it. So much hocus pocus has been built up around

BILL GORMAN

« *People often ask me why I hunt more than I fish. When I was eight, I went fly fishing with my dad. He was sitting in front of me in the boat, and he handed me the rod and said, "Do you want to give this a whirl?" On my first or second false cast, I pierced his ear. We went back to camp so my mom could clip the hook and take it out. I don't think he allowed me to touch a fly rod again until I was fifteen.*

the term "balanced tackle" that the average fisherman is bewildered when it comes to selecting a line.

I have employed the services of an expert in designing the line chart shown below and after having tested it thoroughly I am satisfied that it comes the nearest to being correct of anything I have seen so far.

L.L. BEAN

BILL GORMAN

» *The letters in this table referred to the taper profile. Lines are now numbered, based on the weight in grains of the first thirty feet of line. Generally, you achieve a matching outfit by getting a line and a rod with the same number ("weight") designation.*

Rod Length	Rod Weight	Medium Action Rods			Stiff Action Rods		
		Level	Taper	Torpedo Taper	Level	Taper	Torpedo Taper
7½'	2½-3½ ozs.	E	HDH	HDH	E	HDH	HDH
8'	3½-4½	D	HDH	HCF	D	HDH	HCF
8½'	4½ - 5	D	HDH	HCF	D	HCH	GBF
9'	5-6	D	HCH	GBF	D	HCH	GBF
9½'	6-7	D	HCH	GBF	D	GBG	GBF
10'	7-9	D	GBG	GBF	D	GBG	GAF
11'	10-11	C	GBG	GBF	C	GAG	GAF
12'	11 and up	C	GBG	GBF	C	GAG	GAF

— CHAPTER 24 —

Fishing for Brook Trout with Dry Flies

Walk slowly upstream. If you see a large pool ahead, approach it carefully. Do not stand so that the sun will cause your shadow to fall on the trout's haunts. Make as little noise as possible.

Make your casts so that the fly will land lightly on the water, for you are attempting with artificial lures to attract trout that are accustomed to natural food which they have in abundance during the Summer. Casts of 25 or 30 feet are easier to make and usually will produce more trout than long and difficult casts.

Always be ready for a strike. You must set the hook instantly when fishing with dry flies for brook trout, because the little fellows are gifted with the ability of sampling your attraction and discarding it about as

SPRING 1937

L.L.BEAN Inc.

Parmacheene Belle   Black Gnat   Montreal

Grey Hackle   Scarlet Ibis   Royal Coachman

Brown Hackle   Parmacheene Beau   Silver Doctor

"Nine flies are all anyone needs for Brook Trout. If Trout won't take one of these they aren't rising."

L.L. Bean

fast as you can wink an eye. Large brook trout have a tendency to "bore down" with a fly and you have more time to set your hook properly.

Do not allow the fly to sink. Don't create a disturbance by jerking a fly through or under the water. Your business is to interest a trout enough for him to leave his resting place in an eddy, or behind a rock or sunken log.

Brook trout lay headed upstream, on the lookout for natural food. It sees anything that is in front or at a quartering angle. It is useless to cast behind a trout.

Use flies that look "alive." When it hits the water it should not look like a dead insect.

Although you will find that you have better luck fishing upstream, it is

"It is no longer necessary for you to experiment with dozens of flies," claimed the catalog copy for Bean's nine selected patterns. L.L. had done the work for you.

Opposite: Though many of these flies are no longer available, L.L.Bean still sells the Gray Ghost and Black Gnat flies listed here.

not unusual to fish downstream to good advantage when conditions warrant same, and this is a matter which demands personal judgment.

If you are on a fairly wide stream and you see a pool that looks good, wade slowly out and make frequent short casts. If you are on a stream that has been fished hard, it is often a good plan to sit down occasionally near the largest pools. Enjoy your pipe and watch for the rise of a trout, for when you see one there is an incentive to the sport. You know that it depends on your own ability to inveigle the little fellow again to the surface.

— CHAPTER 25 —

Fly Fishing- Flies and Lures

Lake Trout and Landlocked Salmon. Streamer flies prove efficient in either shallow or deep water. The flies that I have found most effective in the following order are: Supervisor, Red and White Bucktail, Gray Ghost, Green King, Edson Tiger Light, Edson Tiger Dark, Mickey Finn, Parmacheene, Bolshevik, White Bucktail, Brown Bucktail. For trolling I recommend live bait fly as shown on page 51.

Bass: The following flies are okay for bass fishing: Col. Fuller, Parmacheene Belle, Scarlet Ibis, Montreal, Brown Hackle, Gray Hackle. Try a small spinner with these flies. Take along a fly rod mouse and give it a trial when the other lures fail.

COL. FULLER   PARMACHEENE BELLE   SCARLET IBIS   MONTREAL   BROWN HACKLE   GRAY HACKLE

Pickerel. A small spoon and a bright fly is excellent for pickerel. A white and red, or a yellow and red fly with weedless attachment is preferable. Often a small spinner with a piece of pork rind will prove effective.

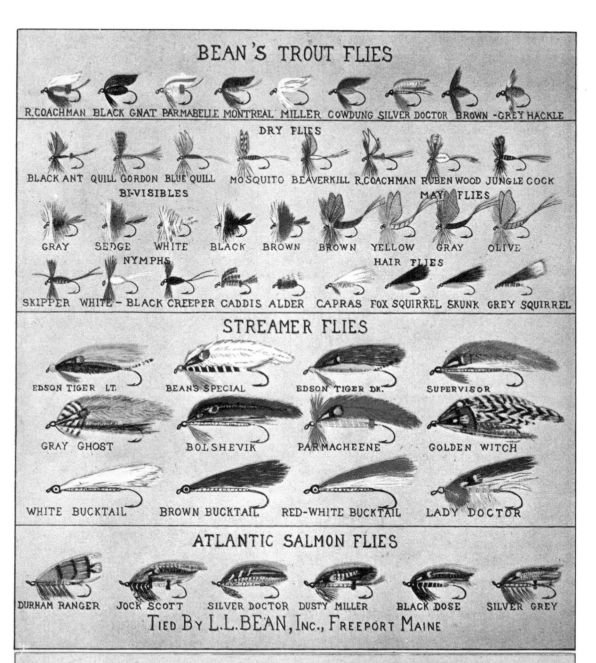

BEAN'S TROUT FLIES

R. COACHMAN BLACK GNAT PARMABELLE MONTREAL MILLER COWDUNG SILVER DOCTOR BROWN GREY HACKLE

DRY FLIES

BLACK ANT QUILL GORDON BLUE QUILL MOSQUITO BEAVERKILL R. COACHMAN RUBEN WOOD JUNGLE COCK

BI-VISIBLES

MAY FLIES

GRAY SEDGE WHITE BLACK BROWN BROWN YELLOW GRAY OLIVE

NYMPHS

HAIR FLIES

SKIPPER WHITE BLACK CREEPER CADDIS ALDER CAPRAS FOX SQUIRREL SKUNK GREY SQUIRREL

STREAMER FLIES

EDSON TIGER LT. BEANS SPECIAL EDSON TIGER DK. SUPERVISOR

GRAY GHOST BOLSHEVIK PARMACHEENE GOLDEN WITCH

WHITE BUCKTAIL BROWN BUCKTAIL RED-WHITE BUCKTAIL LADY DOCTOR

ATLANTIC SALMON FLIES

DURHAM RANGER JOCK SCOTT SILVER DOCTOR DUSTY MILLER BLACK DOSE SILVER GREY

TIED BY L.L. BEAN, INC., FREEPORT MAINE

All our flies, leaders and snelled hooks are tied in our own factory. Prices and Description on pages 3, 4 and 5. Should you come to Maine we extend to you a cordial invitation to visit us in Freeport. Our factory is on Route one, 18 miles East of Portland.

67

SILVER GREY   JOCK SCOTT   SILVER DOCTOR   BLACK DOSE

Atlantic Salmon. For Atlantic Salmon the four flies that I have found most effective in the following order are the Silver Gray, Jock Scott, Silver Doctor and Black Dose, double hooks. For Spring or high water fishing the larger size hooks are best, and I recommend size 1, 2 and 4, double hooks. For low or very clear water, double hooks size 6, 8 and 10.

I recommend double hooks as both Mrs. Bean and I have been very successful taking Atlantic Salmon on the Tobique and Restigouche Rivers. We use double hooks exclusively. See pages 51 and 94.

Brook Trout. For early spring fishing large trout flies are generally the most effective such as the Parmacheene Belle, Silver Doctor, Royal Coachman and White Miller. Also at this time trout will take Nymphs fished near the bottom. As soon as the water drops and becomes warmer the darker and smaller patterns are recommended such as Brown and Grey Hackle, Montreal, Cowdung and Black Gnat.

As soon as natural insects begin to appear in numbers that is the time to change to the Bivisibles and dry flies will take fish through the warm summer months. «

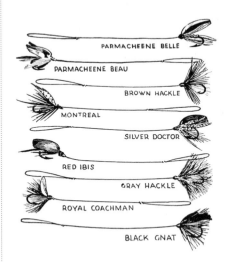

PARMACHEENE BELLE
PARMACHEENE BEAU
BROWN HACKLE
MONTREAL
SILVER DOCTOR
RED IBIS
GRAY HACKLE
ROYAL COACHMAN
BLACK GNAT

BILL GORMAN
» *Fashions have certainly changed since L.L.'s time. While you'll still find Mickey Finns and Gray Ghosts in many fly boxes, you're more likely to see emergers like the Deep Sparkle Pupa that imitate insects reaching their adult stage, weighted nymphs made from synthetic materials, such as the popular Copper John series, and streamers tied with deer or rabbit hair like the Muddler Minnow and its many variants.*

CHAPTER 26

Camping - How to Choose a Tent

When you purchase a tent, get one that is not too large or too small. When you decide on size, type and weight, you must take into consideration the number of people in your party and the method of transporting your outfit and supplies.

Two adults are enough to house in any tent with the exception of an extra large one, although a tent of medium size will often accommodate two adults and one or two children.

For general camping there are three styles of tents which are the most useful, these being the wall, the so-called umbrella or marquee, and the cruiser's or hiker's models. Each has its purpose.

I recommend the wall tent if you can handle its transportation. One large enough to accommodate a camp stove is the most desirable.

For added comfort a canvas floor and fly are well worth taking along. The fly will offer protection against sun and rain, and the floor will keep

Left: Two practical tents with deer in yard. This is a Summer scene. However, don't expect to find deer in your front yard after the season opens.

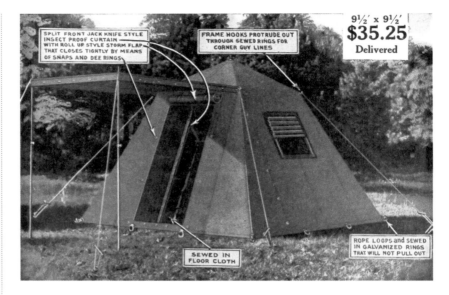

the inside of your tent cleaner and warmer. Removable floor is best, because it can be taken out and cleaned.

The umbrella tent is popular with motor-campers, and most campers prefer the poleless type with sewed-in floor. It requires but little space when packed and is easy to erect. Buy one that is equipped with curtains for they provide ventilation which is so necessary during the warmer months of the year.

The hiker's model is all right for canoe and hiking trips where weight and space is at a premium. A tent of this type is easy to erect and take down. Choose one with a sewed-in floor of canvas. «

— CHAPTER 27 —

Camping - Selecting a Camp Site

When selecting a place to erect your tent, make certain that you are near good drinking water and ample fuel.

Remove rocks and tree limbs from the space you select to set your tent. Don't pitch your tent among large trees, especially trees that are rotten.

Choose a place where water will run away from the tent as much as possible. After your tent is erected, dig a small trench around it about three

BILL GORMAN

» *Outfitters still use heavy wall tents, which are left in place for the season. They are used not unlike cabins. Most people don't camp this way anymore, however. Tents, even the big ones used by car campers, are considerably lighter and easier to set up. Made of waterproof nylons and polyesters, they have free-standing exoskeletons, which allow them to be placed almost anywhere.*

inches deep close to the sidewall. Dig trenches at right angles to the main trench about three feet long and four inches deep to take care of the rain.

See Chapter 36 regarding excellent camp sites in Maine made possible by the Maine Forest Service. Many of these camp sites are located in good hunting and fishing territory, have well-built rock fireplaces and sheltered tables and benches. »

BILL GORMAN
« *L.L.'s recommendations for choice and preparation of campsites was largely dictated by the tents that were available at the time. Most tents were made of canvas, and they had no floor. Digging a trench was the best way to divert rainwater that ran off the tent's sides.*

— CHAPTER 28 —

Camping - How to Erect a Tent

Erecting a tent is a matter of practice. The Cruiser's or Hiker's model is the easiest to erect. Stake down the corners of the floor, adjust the pole and guy lines.

If you use either a Wall tent or an Umbrella tent, I suggest that you erect it in your own back yard previous to a camping trip, so that you will get the "feel" of putting it up correctly.

To erect a Wall tent 9 ½ feet wide and 12 feet long:

First: Drive five stakes down three feet apart.

Second: Opposite and parallel to the stakes, drive another row of stakes, having two rows about 21 feet apart.

Third: Unroll the tent and stretch it out on ground between the two rows of stakes.

Fourth: Attach guy lines loosely to the proper stakes.

Fifth: If the poles are jointed, put the ridge pole in and then one section of the back pole and front pole and repeat the process until tent is up.

Sixth: Peg down all four corners.

Seventh: Adjust guy lines to remove slackness.

It may be necessary to move stacks holding guy lines either toward the tent or away from it, and, if so, remove only one or two stakes at a time while making adjustments.

To erect poleless type Umbrella tent.

First: Open up your tent and secure all corners of the floor with tent pegs.

L.L.BEAN Inc.
Manufacturer
FREEPORT, MAINE
SPRING 1939

Second: Put the top spreading frame together and lay it inside on the floor.

Third: Using one of the corner poles, shove top spreading frame in place, letting the bottom of the pole rest in center of tent.

Fourth: Adjust one corner pole and then the opposite one.

Fifth: Put the third pole in place, remove the pole from the center and put in its proper place at corner.

Sixth: Adjust poles to remove slackness.

Seventh: Outside guy ropes should then be attached to stakes and the canopy poles placed in position.

Eighth: Put canopy up and attach side curtains.

Ninth: Drive all stakes holding guy ropes straight down, not on an angle.

Loosen the guy ropes a little and adjust corner poles if it starts to rain.

— CHAPTER 29 —

Camping - In Old Lumber Camp

There often is good hunting and fishing in the vicinity of abandoned lumber camps, and if the camps are in fair condition a little time and labor is all that is necessary to make at least one of the camps habitable.

Choose one of the smaller buildings for your abode — it probably will

Right: This is a picture of an Old Lumber Camp, which with a little work, makes a comfortable camp.

be the office because it usually is in the best condition.

As the roofs of the camps are often poor, it is advisable to take along a heavy tarpaulin or a tent fly so that you will have a makeshift roof.

You may be lucky and find an old box stove in one of the camps, but the chances are you won't, so it is a good idea to carry along a small folding stove and telescoping stovepipe.

Take along a handful of nails of assorted sizes, plus a small roll of stove-pipe wire, because you will always find such items useful in making an old lumber camp habitable.

You will find good drinking water in the vicinity due to the fact that all lumber camps are constructed near a spring, stream or lake. »

— CHAPTER 30 —

Camping - How to Build a Bough Bed

Cut two logs seven feet long and six or eight inches in diameter. Place the two seven-foot logs parallel to each other and nail the two shorter logs to their ends, making a rough pen to hold boughs. If you haven't nails in your kit cut some pegs or stakes about eight or ten inches long and drive a peg into the ground on each end of each log close to the outer edge. So that the log can't roll outwards when pressure is exerted from within.

Cut some good-sized fir or spruce boughs with your axe. Load the bunk with them. Point all the butts downward into the earth. Then cut a bushel or more of very small fir or balsam boughs. Your sheath knife will do the trick.

Lay the small boughs very carefully on the bunk, starting at the head of the bed. Lay them almost on end, with the under side up.

You will probably run out of boughs by the time you are two-thirds down the bunk, but if the bed is soft and springy under your shoulders and hips, you will sleep okay. If you have plenty of time, cut enough small boughs to finish the bed. »

BILL GORMAN

« *Maine was among the world's biggest suppliers of lumber in the 1800s, and the log buildings that comprised logging camps were scattered throughout the northern woods. By the early- to mid-twentieth century, the abandoned camps had fallen into disrepair, but not so much that they couldn't provide shelter for a hunting party. Most of these camps are gone now, and the ones that are left are private property.*

BILL GORMAN

« *Few people ventured into the wilderness in L.L.'s day, so there was no harm in directing hunters to make a bough bed, which kept sleeping bags dry and provided added insulation. Today, of course, recreational camping is a highly popular activity, and campers are encouraged to minimize their impact on the environment. Fortunately, modern sleeping bags and sleeping pad materials make bough beds unnecessary.*

CHAPTER 31

Camping - Equipment

The best hunting and fishing it often found away from the "beaten trails." What to take to those far-back places depends on the number of people in the party, the duration of the trip, the time of the year and the methods of transportation.

If you travel by Shank's Mare to such locations, or go by canoe, take only the necessities. The list below is intended for two people.

Hiker's or cruiser's tent.

Two sleeping bags.

Large canvas knapsack.

Pack basket with waterproof cover.

Small axe and sheath.

One two-cell flashlight with two extra batteries and one extra bulb.

Folding reflector baker.

Gasoline lantern. (Take candles if transportation is difficult.)

Utensils for cooking and eating should include frying pan, three-quart stew pot with cover, small coffee pot with strainer spout, one stirring spoon, one baker tin, two tin plates, two spoons, two knives, two forks, two cups, salt and pepper shakers.

Auto Camping Equipment

The following list of equipment for auto camping is for two people. If there are more people in the party, you will naturally need more equipment.

Check these items when you pack your equipment in your car at home.

Tent and stakes.

Two folding cots, or two sleeping bags, preferable equipped with air mattresses. Camp cots are cold and uncomfortable without mattresses, especially during the early fishing season and late hunting season.

Air-bed pump.

Strong folding card table.

Bean's pack basket came
in three sizes: boys',
men's, and extra large.
This basket belonged to
a former employee and
was used for camping
from Moosehead Lake
to Alaska.

Two camp stools.

Two reclining camp chairs for relaxation purposes.

A two-burner gasoline stove and a two gallon safety gasoline can.

Two blankets per person if cots are used.

One gasoline lantern. A lighted gasoline lantern resting on the floor of your tent for an hour is ideal for taking off the chill during Spring and early Fall camping.

Cooking and eating utensils should include a heavy gauge 3-quart coffee pot with strainer spout; a 4-quart pail; a medium-sized frying pan; two 2-quart covered pots; reflector baker; long-handled fork; salt and pepper shakers; knife, fork, spoon, cup and plate for each person; one large spoon; one knife with at least an 8-inch blade for cutting meat; one long-handled spoon and one cooking spatula.

One camp axe with sheath.

One small mattock for digging trench around tent.

One flashlight with extra batteries and extra bulbs.

A few nails and a small roll or stovepipe wire will be found useful around camp.

— GEAR, THEN AND NOW —

The biggest change that has occurred in outdoor recreation since L.L. Bean wrote his guide seven decades ago is a cultural one. In the 1940s and 1950s, the woods were the domain of hunters and fishermen, and L.L. directed his advice accordingly. His equipment and grub lists were well suited to a camp that served as a staging area for a multi-day hunt, and, in fact, the provisions are still relevant in the semi-permanent base camps used by today's professional guides and outfitters (if anything, the grub lists might be even more elaborate).

Outdoor recreation, however, has greatly expanded since L.L.'s day. Millions of people spend their weekends and vacations in the woods. For them, camping, canoeing, and hiking are not secondary activities; they are the main events. Gear has evolved to support these ways of enjoying the outdoors, and the trend toward ever-lighter products continues.

The cotton canvas that was once the primary material in tent construction has given way to waterproof nylons and polyesters. Most tents are free-standing, so they can set up on almost any terrain, and they are easily moved without having to be disassembled. The average two-person tent weighs three or four pounds, about one-quarter the weight of a similarly sized tent in L.L.'s day. Likewise, today's sleeping bags are light, waterproof, and compressible into a compact package that is easy to carry on the trail. Self-inflating mattresses serve the same function as L.L.'s bough bed.

The basket-style backpack pictured in Chapter 31 was a practical way to comfortably carry the bulky gear needed to outfit the hunter's base camp. Contemporary backpacks, by contrast, are designed for hiking longer distances and times. Their lightweight internal frames are designed for versatility and to balance load carrying capacity. The gear you put inside it has shrunk: your flashlight is as small and slender as a finger; your stove and cook kit folds up into a package that fits in the palm of your hand.

Car campers, on the other hand, likely have a camping list that is very similar to the one that L.L. devised, right down to the gasoline lantern, but you can leave the ax and mattock at home.

— *Bill Gorman*

CHAPTER 32

Camp Cooking -
How to Use Reflector Baker

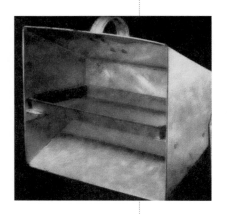

Above: Reflector Bakers come in two models. A non-collapsible as shown, and a collapsible.

BILL GORMAN

» *Professional Maine Guides are known for rustling up multi-course feasts in the wilderness, and the reflector baker is still used by some. Using heat reflected from the campfire, the deceptively simple oven can turn out bread, biscuits, pizza, and just about anything else you'd bake in a home oven, even chocolate chip cookies.*

A reflector baker is one of the most useful equipment items that you can take along on your hunting, fishing and camping trips.

Cooking with a reflector baker is easily learned. If you use the baker outdoors, build a small fireplace or "pen" of stones or green logs. I prefer stones. Select stones about eight or ten inches square that are as flat as you can get in the vicinity, and build a small pen having sides, back and top. Two or three thin stones will suffice for the top, and you may be lucky enough to find one stone that will do the trick. The little pen should be 12 or 14 inches high, 18 inches deep and 12 inches wide.

If you can't find suitable stones for constructing a makeshift fireplace, make one of green logs, splitting those for the top so that your cooking pots will set level.

Build your fire in your fireplace. Place the reflector baker about four inches from the front, so the blaze hits the bottom and reflects upward, also the blaze hits the inside top and reflects down, and you can bake anything that can be baked in an oven. You can regulate heat by moving the baker.

If you use any type of wood-burning stove that doesn't have an oven, place the baker against the side of the stove, as close as possible. With a bit of experimenting, you can use a reflector baker in conjunction with a gasoline stove.

It is possible to bake beans in a reflector baker without interfering with your other duties around camp if you use a wood-burning stove. Lacking a bean pot in your outfit, use a two-quart pail or dish. Soak the beans overnight, and in the morning place in pail, adding two tablespoons of sugar, teaspoon dry mustard, very little salt and pepper, and nearly one pound of salt pork. Now fill pail with water, place on shelf of baker, and place baker against side of stove. «

Ordinarily, half a pound of salt pork is sufficient to use in baking two quarts of beans, but you will find that a pound is better if you are away from camp most of the day and can't attend to your cooking properly. If you plan to be away from camp all day, fill the stove with wood before you leave camp. When you return at night, start your fire and add water to the beans. Add more water before you go to bed. Beans should be well done for one of your meals the next day.

In most states there are public camp sites where fireplaces are built. (See page 85). »

— CHAPTER 33 —

Camp Cooking and Grub Lists

It is difficult to state just what any party should carry into the woods for a fishing, hunting or camping trip. Camper's tastes vary, so there must be some leeway as far as grub lists are concerned, and the method of transportation must also be taken into consideration. Naturally, if you are on a canoe or hiking trip far from grocery stores, you must plan your grub list accordingly, making it light in weight and as compact as possible. On the other hand, if you travel right to your camp door in your auto, you can take along a larger variety of foodstuffs and forget the matter of weight and bulk.

I wish to have it understood that the following suggestions, grub lists and recipes are subject to individual correction. When you look at a list of food to be taken on a trip, eliminate the items which you don't like and substitute other food materials of equal weight. For instance, if you like coffee and not tea, don't take the tea along just because it is on the grub list.

May I suggest that you pack food supplies carefully before leaving for camp. Pack items, such as flour, bacon, salt pork, sugar, oatmeal, rice, beans and cornmeal, in small bags of

BILL GORMAN

« *The right selection of foods is important when participating in strenuous outdoor activities, especially on multi-day trips. High-energy foods like cookies, chocolate, nuts, fruit leathers, trail mix, hard cheese, and salami not only satisfy your body's caloric needs but also pack easily and will keep for a few days. If you're backpacking, consider lightweight (and, these days, surprisingly tasty) boil-in-bag and freeze-dried gourmet dinners, instant cereals and soups, and dried pasta.*

Above: On overnight trips, don't load yourself down.

medium-weight cloth that are equipped with puckering strings. The individual bags should then be placed in slightly larger bags that are waterproofed. The bags may be tagged so that they may easily be identified.

The use of dehydrated foods for camping use is rapidly becoming more popular. Dehydrated vegetables are vegetables with all moisture content removed — they crackle and break in your hand.

Such vegetables as beets, carrots, potatoes, onions, turnips, beans and tomatoes are easy to carry in such a concentrated form. Many of the small packages weigh only 1¾ ounces yet the contents will be found sufficient to make several servings. Such vegetables, being in concentrated form, require no refrigeration.

If you go on overnight trips away from your main camp, don't load yourself down with grub. If there are two in the party, take some sandwiches, 1 package Dehydrated Potatoes, 1 package prepared Pancake Flour, I can Evaporated Milk, 1 pound Bacon, ¼ pound Brown Sugar, a handful of Coffee, 4 Tea Bags, 8 lumps Sugar, ¼ pound Butter and 4 Doughnuts. This is enough grub for four meals.

Carry a combination salt and pepper shaker, a folding handle frying pan, a two-quart pail, 2 knives, 2 forks, 2 spoons, 2 plates and 2 cups. Put all food and cooking and eating utensils in a small knapsack. The total weight of knapsack, cooking and eating utensils and food supplies is less than nine pounds. By using two knapsacks and dividing the load you can hunt or fish, going and coming. If hunting, cover knapsack with red handkerchief.

If you are going hunting, fishing or camping and you want to cook as little as possible, the following grub list will serve your purpose. It is just about right for a party of two adults for six or seven days. It is for those campers who have an opportunity to easily transport their supplies to camp.

4 Loaves Bread

2 Cans Baked Beans

2 Cans of Corned Beef Hash

1 Lb. Coffee

¼ Lb. Tea

2 Lbs. Sugar

1 Bottle Pancake Syrup

2 Packages Prepared Pancake Flour

3 Cans Evaporated Milk

3 Lbs. Flour

3 Lbs. Bacon

1 Doz. Fresh Eggs

1 Can Corn

1 Can Tomatoes

4 Ounces Salt

4 Ounces Soda

2 Lbs. Salt Pork

4x4-oz. cans Dehydrated Potatoes

1 Can Peaches

1 Lb. Butter

1 Small Can Pepper

1 Small Bottle Vinegar

1 Small Jar Mustard

1 Dozen Doughnuts

1 Lb. Cookies

The above grub list may be changed to suit your particular requirements. For instance, some campers make pancake syrup from brown sugar or from cakes of maple sugar.

The flour will be found useful for preparing gravy and for cooking fish. If you plan to be away from camp at lunch time each day, add at least two loaves of bread to the above grub list. Add meat to this list to suit your requirements.

Apples, oranges and other fresh fruit always go well in camp. »

— CHAPTER 34 —

Camp Cooking-Recipes

Venison Steak Cut steak about 1 ½ inches thick. Remove excess fat and wipe clean and dry. Have a very hot fire and when frying pan is smoking hot drop steak into the pan and allow to sear quickly on one side. Then turn.

If you like steak medium or well done, reduce the heat of the fire and turn occasionally, until at desired stage. If you prefer a rare steak, it will require 10 to 12 minutes; medium, 15 to 20 minutes.

Serve on a hot platter. Spread steak with butter and add salt and pepper to taste.

BILL GORMAN
« *Today you could condense all the food L.L. lists for an overnight trip into two packages. You don't need things like flour, sugar, and butter because they are already in the prepared, dehydrated dinners. You just add water.*

Venison Cutlets Cut small slices of meat from the loin about 1 ¼ inches thick. Sprinkle with salt and pepper and brush with melted butter. Roll in bread crumbs. Fry in butter.

Roast Duck Clean and dress duck. Steam about 1 ½ hours before roasting. Stuff with sliced onion or apple. Sprinkle with salt and pepper and cover breasts with several slices of salt pork. Bake about 20 minutes in a very hot oven, basting every 4 or 5 minutes with fat in pan. Remove stuffing before serving.

Roast Leg of Venison Cut leg and a piece of the loin which will weigh about 5 or 6 pounds. Wipe dry with a damp cloth. Sprinkle lightly with salt and pepper and roll in flour. Attach several strips of salt pork or bacon. Put in roaster and bake three hours. «

Fried Grouse Skin and dress the grouse. Remove the legs. Cut breast in half lengthwise. Break down flat the piece containing the breast bone, doing this with a camp axe or back of a hunting knife. Wipe with damp cloth. Fry in pork or bacon fat. Season to taste with salt and pepper when served. «

Roast Pheasant Dress and clean pheasant. Tie several pieces of fat bacon on breasts. Bake 30 to 50 minutes, basting frequently with fat in pan. Remove bacon before serving.

Pea Soup Place one cup of split peas and ham bone in kettle and cover with water. Let simmer until peas and meat are well done, this requiring about 3 hours. Remove the bone and strain peas. Remove bits of meat from bone and add to soup. Thin with milk if too thick. This is enough for four people, one generous serving each. Pea Flour is now available in ¾ ounce packages (one serving). Ready to serve in about 10 minutes.

BILL GORMAN
» *If I had a leg of venison, I would grill it, medium rare. It's healthier and the flavor is better.*

BILL GORMAN
» *One of the highlights of hunting as a teenager was my mother's cooking. We'd bring home grouse, pheasant, rabbit, even gray squirrel, and she would cook it. She loved it (and she still does).*

This elegant fish knife was a fixture in L.L.Bean's fishing line for forty years, from 1936 until 1976.

CHAPTER 35

Camping Hints

If you take a trip away from the main camp for a day or two, and use either a small tent or a lean-to for shelter, take sugar in lump form, because if you drop some on the ground it is easy to pick up.

If you use a large wall tent or one of the umbrella style, and transportation or equipment and supplies is not too difficult, take along single camp cots for each occupant. A two-burner gasoline stove will be right for camp cooking. And don't forget the gasoline.

A small alarm clock is an asset at any hunting camp.

For real warmth and comfort on the outdoor trails, a sleeping bag is hard to beat. They are excellent on hunting, fishing and camping trips where it is not practical to carry along folding cots, mattresses and blan-

kets. During the summer a piece of cheese cloth sprinkled with kerosene or fly spray is necessary to cover the canopy to keep the black flies, midges and mosquitoes away. If you haven't an air mattress it is a good idea to build a bough bed and place your sleeping bag on it if you desire a real "woodsy" and comfortable bed.

When you get home from a camping trip, take your tent out of its bag and spread it out to dry before storing it away for the winter.

If you lunch along the highway, be sure to pick up all rubbish. If you have a fire put it out with water.

To remove rust, soot and grease from pots and pans, wet a cloth in hot water, dip in wood ashes and scour the utensils by a back-and-forth rubbing motion.

When mosquitoes and black flies are plentiful, I recommend stockings long enough so that pant legs can be tucked inside. This will save you a lot of discomfort.

BILL GORMAN
» *Today, Maine has 424 permit camp sites made available through the Maine Forest Service, and 426 camp sites on public reserve lands, as well as countless others in state parks and elsewhere. You can find information about camping, parks, and much more through the Maine Department of Conservation at maine.gov/doc*

— CHAPTER 36 —

How to Prevent Forest Fires

A large number of forest fires in Maine are caused by careless smokers and campers.

The fire hazard in Maine with its 16,270,000 acres of forest land has become a serious matter.

Maine issued 243,229 hunting and fishing licenses in 1948. This army of hunters, fisherman and campers can be a great help to prevent forest fires.

In 1944 forest fires in Maine burned over 24,203 acres. »

The opportunities for recreation, sport and other out-of-door activities as offered in certain sections of this State, will no longer be available if fires are allowed to claim their heavy toll.

To help check this yearly loss, hunters, fisher-men and campers should observe and put into practice a few simple forest fire protection rules as follows:

Rake away all inflammable material before lighting the fire.

Don't toss your match away — break it in two, step on it, and be sure it is out.

Don't throw cigarette butts from an automobile window.

Never build a fire against a log, tree or stump.

Never leave a fire burning or try to kick it out.

Pour plenty of water on your fire, or use plenty of dirt.

When you think it is out, feel it with your hands to make sure.

(A fire is never out until the last spark has been extinguished).

If a fire gets beyond your control, call the nearest Fire Warden or Lookout Station.

Maine now has about 200 camp sites made possible by the Maine Forest Service where natives and non-residents may kindle fires without penalty or without being accompanied by a registered guide. (They are for temporary use). Parties using these sites are requested to use care in disposal of refuse and to take precautions against possible contamination of the water supply. Each party, upon vacating, is requested to put out his fire with water, remove all tents or shelters and pick up all rubbish. «

BILL GORMAN
« In 1947, a series of fires burned between 175,000 and 200,000 acres of woodland and destroyed nearly half of Mount Desert Island.

BILL GORMAN

» *During the thirties and forties, sportsmen built campfires for warmth and cooking. Thanks to advances in camping gear, campfires are rarely a necessity anymore, though they are very popular. Some wilderness lands are so heavily used by campers that their forest floors have been picked clean of fallen branches, and campfires are not permitted at all.*

These Camp Sites are all located along well-traveled roads, trails and streams, and handy to a supply of water.

The Maine Highway Department will supply maps, which show the location of these to any interested party.

Whenever you camp, be sure your fire is out before you leave.

A good many fires could be avoided if the smoker would only stop to think and see that his match, cigarette, cigar stub or pipe ashes is entirely out.

The forests are the greatest heritage that was ever given to the people of Maine. It is hoped that smokers and fishermen will always be mindful of helping to keep them green. When fires destroy the forests around the head waters of small trout streams, the little spring feeders dry up and many trout die for want of water.

Broken bottles or broken glass left in the woods by picnic parties and transients can develop a cause of forest fires. Curved pieces of glass can intensify the rays of the sun shining on them to the point where fire can ignite the dry leaves, duff or humus beneath.

The best time to stop a forest fire is just before you start it. A Fire-Proof forest demands one-hundred percent public cooperation. Wild Life depends on the forests. Keep Them Green. «

— CHAPTER 37 —

Where and When to Go Hunting and Fishing

If you want to go deer hunting in Maine, you will find a map on page 106 of this Book showing where every deer was shot in 1941. «

Ask the Maine Department of Inland Fisheries and Wildlife when the first snow is expected and be on the spot when it comes. Of course you may miss the snow but at that time of year the leaves are well off and you are almost sure to get *rain* or snow so that you can get around quietly. The weather will be much better for keeping game than earlier in the season. If you *do* get a light snow fall, without crust, hunting conditions will be perfect. »

BILL GORMAN

» *For the 2010 Deer Kill Map see page 108, and for more information get in touch with the State of Maine Department of Inland Fisheries and Wildlife: maine.gov/ifw.*

If you want to go fishing in Maine, a great deal depends on the time you can get away. As a general rule, the later in the season the farther North you will need to go. For example, Sebago Lake is fair fishing up to July 1st. Moosehead Lake is very fair up to August 1st and Rangeley Lakes are about in between. If you go later than August 1st you should pick your location very carefully. You may find it necessary to go way back on small streams or ponds.

Write the MDIF&W the date you want to go and the makeup of your party. There are a number of places where you can get fair fishing right up until the season closes, but the chances are you will be obliged to do quite a great deal of walking.

When writing the MDIF&W, insist on detail information regarding the section of the State in which you are interested. See maps on pages 106, 107 and 108. »

BILL GORMAN
« *Scout areas before deciding where to hunt. Today we often go out pre-season, look for signs of deer activity, and strap a motion-activated game camera to a tree so we know where to set up our tree stand.*

BILL GORMAN
« *Today, you can locate detailed fishing reports quickly on the Internet. The Maine Department of Inland Fisheries and Wildlife has lots of useful information for anglers: maine.gov/ifw/fishing*

Your Guide

BILL GORMAN

» *By "cold country," L.L. is probably referring to Canada. The last confirmed sighting of caribou in Maine was in 1908. Two efforts to restore the animals to the state — one in 1963, the other in 1989 — failed.*

BILL GORMAN

» *I hunt more than most people, but if I'm going somewhere new, I still think it is advantageous to hire a guide. The first time you hunt a new animal, or in a new state, a guide will show you where the animals are and what their practices are. This gives you more time to hunt and helps support the local economy. Visit the Maine Professional Guides Association Website at maineguides.org.*

If you employ a guide on a hunting trip, I recommend that you have him carry a lightweight, full size axe, instead of a gun, also a very small pack sack with food enough for three meals, tin dishes for two, a small pail for making tea and a small fry pan.

In case of accident or other reasons you are obliged to stay out over night you will find one gun and one axe much better than two guns.

With an axe you can build a lean-to, get wood and make a fairly comfortable bed. In 1926 I was Caribou hunting in a very cold country. «

My guide carried an axe instead of a gun, also the other things mentioned above. We had a good hot meal every day at noon time. I was so impressed with the idea that I have never allowed my guide to carry a gun since, except to help hunt down a wounded deer. Years ago when my guide carried a gun duck hunting, I never knew who shot the ducks. Now my guide attends to the sculling and I handle the gun. If a duck drops, I know who shot it.

You may be invited to make a party of four who make a practice of having cocktails, playing cards in camp and letting the guide shoot the deer. Don't accept the invitation. Learn to shoot your own deer. It will be a great deal more satisfactory. The open air and exercise is well worth your time even if you fail to get your deer.

The State of Maine has Class A and Class B Guides. The Inland Fish and Game laws provide, that "No person shall be issued a Class A guide's certificate unless he is physically, mentally and morally capable of guiding and caring for a party anywhere in the forests or on the waters of the State." «

— THE MAINE GUIDE TRADITION —

If you're heading into the Maine wilderness for the first time, you would do well to hire a guide who knows the area and has earned the trust of others in the field. A Registered Maine Guide has successfully passed some of the most rigorous wilderness guide licensing programs in the country. He or she can help you optimize your experience, be it hunting, fishing, trapping, boating, snowmobiling, or primitive camping.

The legendary Cornelia "Fly Rod" Crosby received the first Maine guiding license on March 19, 1897. For many years, Registered Maine Guides primarily served hunters and fishermen, and they earned their license simply by proving their mettle to the local game warden. In 1975, the Maine Warden Service instituted a standardized test that includes a written and an oral examination. The program places a premium on safety, and registered guides have demonstrated, among other things, that they know how to react quickly and with a good plan should a client become lost. Registered Maine Guides are well versed in fishing, hunting, trapping laws, and other rules governing outdoor recreation.

In addition to the regular license, a master certification is available to guides who demonstrate a high level of experience and skill in certain areas, such as hunting, fishing, sea kayaking, and other activities.

By hiring a Registered Maine Guide for your first outing in a new area, you not only will improve your odds of catching fish or getting game, you'll likely be treated to an outstanding meal. Registered Maine Guides are nearly as well known for their delicious spreads — roasted chicken, savory baked salmon, fresh biscuits, even pineapple upside down cake — as they are for their wilderness expertise. — *Bill Gorman*

1926 SPRING SUPPLEMENT

L. L. Bean, Manufacturer
FREEPORT, MAINE

CHAPTER 39

General Information

BILL GORMAN

» *L.L. was always likeable. I remember being five years old and sitting on L.L.'s lap, stitching a pair of Maine hunting shoes. I'd hate to be the customer that got that pair, but L.L. was always patient and loved to have us take part in the tradition.*

When on your hunting trips do not try to belittle the back woods folk even though you are a college man and your home is in a big city.

While your education and personal appearance may be far superior to theirs, they may be getting just as much pleasure out of life as yourself and when it comes right down to country common sense, they probably have you beaten.

A few years ago a New Jersey nimrod, while fishing in Northern Maine got mixed up in his direction while attempting a shortcut to camp. He finally ran into a barefoot boy and started asking him questions without admitting the fact that he did not know the way home. Unable to get an intelligent reply that would help him out of his predicament he finally said, "I guess you don't know much anyway, do you?" The boy answered. "No, but I'm not lost."

Last Fall we received from our good friend, Robert B. Summers, a letter as follows:

"The Summer of 1949 my wife and I were vacationing on a small island off the Maine coast, called Vinalhaven. There was an old man who lived alone on the Northeast tip of this island, sort of isolated from the rest of the natives. We always made it a practice to call on this old man while we were there. He was so pleasant and very highly educated. So one day while we were making a call some young summer people from New York City were out hiking around the island. They had lost their way back and

L. L. Bean, Inc.
Spring 1972

stopped at this old man's house to inquire their way home. Before they left they said to the old man, 'Do you know, Mister, there are some queer people on this island.'

"The old man says, 'Yes, I know there are, young man, but they will all be gone by Labor Day.'" «

Summer Care of Snowshoes

Wipe clean and varnish both the wood and webbing. Any high grade spar-varnish will do. Two coats are better than one, but in any case, they should be thin coats.

Tie the shoes securely together, back to back, and force block of wood into the space between the toes.

Place them out of the sun and hang by the tail. Suspend by wire so that mice or squirrels cannot get at them.

You may be the big toad in the puddle when you are home but don't try to poke fun at the "Small Town" folk until you are sure you are "out of the woods."

There are about twenty-three million hunters in the United States. Therefore, when you will go fishing or hunting do not set your expectations too high. You may fish all day and not get a strike. You may hunt all day and not even see a deer. In fact you may go home empty-handed. Therefore, make up your mind to have a good time. Enjoy camp life and exercise in the open air and you will be well repaid for your trip. I have hunted three days without seeing a deer. On the forth day I had my deer hung up and was spotting a trail back to camp before 9 A.M.

To be a successful hunter or fisherman you must have a great deal of patience. »

L. L. Bean Inc.
Spring 1943

BILL GORMAN
« *The hunt is just not about the kill. It's also about enjoying the outdoors. I've seen hawks land five feet from me. I've had songbirds hop up and down on my arrow. I even had one peck on my hand. Just watching all that activity is satisfying. If you're successful in the hunt as well, that's fantastic.*

— CONSERVATION SUCCESSES —

Between its forests, mountains, water bodies, wetlands, coastline, and islands, Maine is blessed with a rich diversity of habitat and wildlife species. Naturally, a priority of the Maine Department of Inland Fisheries and Wildlife (MDIF&W) is to maintain that diversity and conserve the state's resources for future generations. It does this through wise use and proper management, and its job of balancing the needs of various parties interested in wildlife is not easy.

Through the years the state has enjoyed a number of conservation success stories worth telling.

Moose

According to early explorers, moose were plentiful in New England in the 1600s. By the early 1900s, however, Maine's moose population had declined to about two thousand. Excessive hunting was mostly to blame, with additional factors being clearing forestland for farms and increased incidence of fatal brainworm because of increasing numbers of deer (deer are carriers of brainworm, but do not suffer the ill effects).

Moose seasons varied in length and bag limit and were closed periodically. In 1936 the season was closed again, and it remained closed until 1980. That year seven hundred permits were issued to Maine residents for a six-day, September season, and 635 moose were taken. Following that, carefully controlled hunts were held on an annual basis, and moose numbers were monitored closely. In 2010, 3,188 permits were issued for four different seasons, and 2,393 moose were taken. The state's moose population currently stands above 29,000, which, according to state wildlife managers, is a healthy population for the amount of moose habitat that is available in the state.

Wild Turkeys

Due mostly to extensive land clearing for farming and unrestricted shooting, wild turkeys were virtually eliminated in Maine in the early 1800s. Several attempts to reintroduce turkeys to the state were made in the 1940s and '60s, but it wasn't until 1977, when Maine Department of Inland Fisheries and Wildlife biologists took forty-one turkeys that had been trapped in Vermont and released them in York County, that the birds began to take hold. Since then, thanks to in-state trap-and-transplant efforts and the release of an additional forty turkeys from Connecticut in the late 1980s, the population of Maine's largest game bird has taken off. Today estimates put the state's turkey population at between 50,000 and 60,000 birds, and state wildlife managers have achieved about 90 percent of their goal of having viable turkey numbers wherever suitable habitat exists.

Whitetail Deer

Conservation success doesn't always mean having the largest population of a particular species. Numbers need to be balanced with habitat.

For the past four hundred years, whitetail deer numbers have fluctuated based on land-use practices, predation, climate change, and disturbances like wildfires and floods. The state has been regulating deer hunting since 1830, when it implemented the first season (with no bag limit). Since then the state has been tweaking seasons, limits, and other regulations in order to try to reach management goals. Peak harvests occurred in the 1950s, when the state was wintering about 275,000 whitetails and either-sex hunting regulations were in effect.

More recently, harvests have been lower, but this can be attributed to not only fewer deer, but also fewer hunters. In addition, increasing development in some areas has necessitated switching from firearms hunting to bowhunting only.

In the past couple of years, deer numbers in northern, eastern, and western Maine have been estimated at 200,000 - 255,000, below the goals of the MDIF&W as well as the expectations of hunters. As a result, significant efforts are being made to restore populations in those areas. This is a long-term project, but if the track record of the department is any indication, chances are good that sportsmen and other wildlife enthusiasts will have another conservation success story to tell.

— *Bill Gorman*

CHAPTER 40

Atlantic Salmon Fishing

The Atlantic Salmon is without a doubt the scrappiest fish that can be taken on a fly. They care caught to some extent in Maine but at present the choicest fishing is in the eastern provinces of Canada and in Newfoundland.

The Atlantic Salmon migrate from the sea to the cold rivers to spawn, but, unlike their Pacific brothers, they do not die afterwards and often live to ten years during which time they will spawn as many as three times. The salmon always returns to the same river where he was hatched.

Nothing but fly fishing is permitted in the rivers. Contrary to general belief no fancy or special tackle is necessary. Your stiff fly rod and your

Right: Taking five salmon in a single day, L.L. Bean, of Freeport, Saturday broke the record for the famous Plaster Rock Pool in the Tobique River in New Brunswick. Mr. Bean, shown above with his record day's catch, also set another unusual record by taking each fish on a different pattern of salmon fly. The fish, which weighed from 8 ½ to 9 ½ pounds each, were all landed on a 5 ½ ounce rod.

ordinary fly line will do nicely except that you should splice fifty yards of 18 pound test line and have a reel large enough to carry it.

Numerous salmon flies are offered but the most popular are Silver Gray, Silver Doctor, Jock Scott, and Black Dose in the order listed. The camp where you are staying usually supplies the gaff or net.

Fishing can be done by wading, but on larger rivers, the canoe is more popular as it can be poled up stream and more water can be covered on the way down. A guide is necessary to handle the canoe.

Plenty of time should be taken in fishing so all the water is covered as a salmon's eyesight is none too good and they will seldom strike when farther than six feet from the fly.

Salmon fishing differs from trout fishing in one important respect in that under no circumstances should you hold a looped line in the left hand while the fly is on the water. If you do and a salmon strikes he will either tear the fly out or break your leader. There will be no doubt about it when he strikes and no effort should be made to "horse" him in for you simply cannot do it.

While some fishermen prefer the early mornings and later evenings for salmon fishing, just as many fish have been hooked at mid-day. Like other fish they take more readily on a changing temperance, which always follows a rise or fall of the water.

Unlike most fish, salmon will not always strike a fly on the first cast. The author knows of one case where seventy-two casts were made in one spot over a salmon before he took the fly.

If the fisherman prefers to equip himself with special salmon tackle, I recommend a seven or eight ounce rod with a detachable butt. A triple tapered line of the "Torpedo Taper" variety with one hundred yards of eighteen pound test backing line. A reel with drag and large enough to hold the extra line. Leaders should be at least eight feet long and test about 10 lbs. A landing net about 17" x 18" at top and 36" deep with handle six feet long. »

L.L.Bean®
Spring 1983

BILL GORMAN
« *Given decades of habitat degradation (both in salmon natal watersheds in Maine and on the high seas), as well as overharvesting, in 2000 Atlantic salmon populations in eight Maine rivers (Cove Brook, Dennys, Ducktrap, East Machias, Machias, Narraguagus, Pleasant, and Sheepscot) were declared federally endangered. As of this writing, fishing for Atlantic salmon in Maine waters is prohibited.*

CHAPTER 41

Canoeing

If you intend to use your canoe on swift water as well as lakes and ponds, a twenty-foot Guide's Model is best. If the canoe is to be used only on lakes and ponds, a canoe of the same size with keel is preferable.

Two paddles, one 5 ½ feet long and the other 6 feet, are necessary. Use paddles of seasoned maple or ash with well-shaped blade and shank.

For quick water work you should have a good spruce pole 11 or 12 feet long and 2 inches in diameter, equipped with an iron socket on one end. A sponge for removing water and about 30 feet of strong clothesline is almost a necessity.

The pole is indispensable for going up swift streams where a paddle is useless. For going down stream, a pole is necessary to snub the canoe.

When going up a very fast stream where a pole cannot be used, attach one end of the clothesline to the bow of the canoe and walk along the bank of the stream and tow the craft as best you can. Let your companion keep the bow off shore with aid of the pole. There are many streams too swift for the proper use of a line, necessitating carrying the canoe around such

Right: Warden Bert Duty poling over a dam on Mud Pond Stream, Maine.

SPRING 1938

L.L.BEAN Inc. MANUFACTURER FREEPORT MAINE

Left: The most practical canoe for Maine Lakes and general canoe trips is the 20 ft. Guide model.

rapids. Before using a canoe in quick water, fill it with water and let it soak on hour or two. A canoe that is very dry is apt to be brittle.

The best way to learn how to properly handle a canoe is to go canoeing with a person who is familiar with such a craft. You will learn how to handle the bow paddle first, then the stern, and later use of the pole. If you don't have an instructor, I suggest that for practice purposes you put two or three rocks in the bow. The total weight of the rocks should be at least 100 pounds. Choose a calm day for your first few practice lessons, and stay on a lake, pond or river where there is only a little current.

Paddle in easy, steady strokes, with one hand just above the blade and

Above: Poling canoe on dry land at Mud Pond Carry Tramway.

BILL GORMAN
» *Wooden canoes today are a niche product for wooden boat aficionados who admire their beauty, craftsmanship, as well as their functionality. Most paddlers opt for lighter vessels and paddles made of fiberglass, high-impact plastic, or Kevlar. Kayaks, which are faster and easier to maneuver, are equally popular.*

other on the handle. Don't try to reach out too far and attempt to make extra-long strokes. Steering a canoe without paddling on one side and then the other is mastered by a little practice.

You can go down many streams without using a pole, but I do not suggest it unless you know the streams well and also are aware of all the hidden rocks and sunken logs that might capsize your canoe if hit.

Take good care of your canoe. Don't pull or push a canoe around the beach the way some folks handle rowboats. Carry a repair kit and examine your canoe daily while in use and repair all rips and tears.

Balancing of load in the canoe is very important. The heaviest of duffle must, by necessity, be in the center.

In running white water the load should balance slightly in back of center to allow the canoe to be swung or set instantly. «

— CHAPTER 42 —

Salt Water Fishing

I should not consider my book complete without a word about Salt Water Fishing.

In recent years, Maine has added salt water fishing for giant bluefin tuna, striped bass and mackerel.

The best spot for tuna fishing is in the Bailey Island area of Casco Bay where these giant fish run from 200 lbs. up to over 700.

Regulation big game, deep sea fishing outfits are necessary to handle these giant bluefins, with the minimum tackle being 16 oz. tips, at least 500 yards of 24-thread line, and 10/0 reel.

For the beginner, I recommend 36-thread line and a 14/0 reel, also that you hire a regular fishing boat that is fully equipped for taking out parties. After fishing a season or two, you might want to own your own boat. The best season is late July to mid-September. Due to recent increases in striped bass, anglers have found that Maine can produce plenty of activity for the thousands of salt water anglers who look upon striped bass as one of the finest light tackle salt water fish. One of the most reliable lures for stripers is the sea-worm, (sometimes called blood worm) either with or without sinker or spinner or trolling with a smooth running spinner baited with sea-worms. Although most of Maine's best striped bass fishing is in the tidal waters of its streams, these fish can also be taken surf casting, and here a regulation surf-casting outfit is in order. Best season is from late June through September. »

BILL GORMAN
« *Striped bass fishing was just catching on when L.L. wrote his guide, but by the late 1970s, stripers had all but disappeared due to overfishing and habitat degradation. Strict management has since brought the population back to sustainable levels.*

Another form of salt water fishing that has gained great favor with fly fishermen is fly fishing for mackerel. Although small, seldom exceeding a pound in weight, these trim torpedoes strike eagerly at streamer and bucktail flies and, "ounce for ounce," are worthy of the skill of any fly fisherman. »

BILL GORMAN
« *When he was older, L.L. often went down to Florida. One time he caught a swordfish that he sent back to the store to be mounted. The employees thought he sent it for them to enjoy. They ate his trophy fish!*

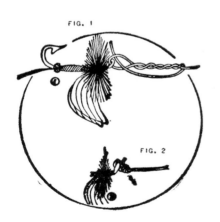

FIG. 1

FIG. 2

"Clinch Knot" for Fishing Leaders

One of the best known knots for nylon leaders is illustrated at the left. Stick the end of the tippet through the eye of the fly, double it back against itself for four or five inches, give the fly several complete twists to wind the leader spirally around itself four or five times as shown in Figure I.

Thrust the end between the eye and coils, hold on to it, and pull up tightly and securely as shown in Figure II.

Baxter State Park

Below: Hon. Percival P. Baxter, Former Governor of Maine.
Opposite: Chimney Pond and the East wall of Katahdin, showing inside of "Chimney."

While I have made this book primarily one of practical information for hunting, fishing and camping, I cannot close without a brief chapter on Maine's unspoiled wilderness reservation, and the State's greatest benefactor, former Governor Percival P. Baxter, the man who literally has given away mountains. «

Baxter State Park covers 254 square miles of forest, 162,939 acres.

So much of Maine is wooded, ranging from small, upland growth to heavy, sometimes almost impenetrable, forests, that some might think of a state park designed to preserve the forest lands as fairly redundant.

But forests, if not protected, eventually succumb to the steady inroads of lumbering and other commercial activities. Knowing that, a former Governor of Maine has created a state park so that natives and summer tourists may always enjoy one section of the state in its wild, natural condition.

Mr. Baxter undertook creation of the state park back in 1930 and has individually purchased every inch of that vast domain to make it possible, presenting thousands of acres to the state. Today Baxter State Park is the third largest in the country, only New York and California boasting larger ones.

That the park is becoming more and more popular with tourists, despite the fact it is not as heavily publicized as some other attractions, is shown by the steadily rising figures for visitors — 7,000 in 1948 and 10,000 in 1949.

Baxter Park has twenty-six mountain peaks in it, ranging from 2,306 feet up. Their heights, of course, do not approach those to be found in other parts of the country, but many of them loom relatively high above the surrounding land. And Mount Katahdin, 5,267 feet above sea level at its peak, is actually higher from base to summit than New Hampshire's Mount Washington. The highest peak, by Legislative Act is named "Baxter Peak."

L. L. Bean, Inc.
Spring 1973

Katahdin is king of the region, and one of the most striking mountains in the country. It has been called "the distinctist mountain to be found on this side of the continent" — a reference to the way it looms almost alone out of the spruce and fir forests. Katahdin is a mountain rich in Indian legend, particularly in stories of Pamola, the mountain deity, who was so wrathful that he destroyed any Indian who came near his summit.

For those who feel no special urge to climb a mountain "because it is there," a good reason for climbing Katahdin can still be advanced. It provides magnificent views. The mountain itself is far more rugged and sharply cut by glacial action than most other Eastern peaks.

Above the timber line is a vast sea of boulders cut by sharp granite ridges. Henry David Thoreau, who visited it in 1846, said it was "as if at some time it had rained rocks and they lay as they fell on the mountain, nowhere fairly at rest, but leaning on each other, all rocking-stones, with cavities between, but scarcely any soil or smoother shelf."

Right: Katahdin Campsite at the foot of Hunt Trail, Baxter Park.

There are several trails up Katahdin and none of them is a quiet promenade. The easiest is the Hunt Trail, northernmost five miles of the Maine-to-Georgia Appalachian Trail. This includes a long, gradual woodland ascent, a quick scramble over immense boulders with the aid of iron handles fixed to the rock, and a gentle climb over the boulder-strewn plateau to the summit. This trail is well marked and can be negotiated by inexperienced but sure-footed climbers.

The most spectacular trail on Katahdin in the Knife Edge. This follows a narrow, humping ridge that walls off the glacial Great Basin on the north from the southern slope of the mountain. At many points the ridge is only about a yard wide, with a 1,500 foot drop on each side. When the wind blows there is an overwhelming temptation just to lie down and hug the surface. The Knife Edge can be dangerous, and should be attempted only in perfect weather.

Another of the taller mountains in Baxter State Park is Traveler, 4,000 feet high, where, it is believed, more moose roam than in any comparable area in the country. Caribou disappeared from the area in 1901, but it is hoped the moose, on which there is a closed season, lifted only at long intervals by special act of the Legislature, will never be killed off by hunters.

Hunting is prohibited throughout the state park, although fishing is allowed. At the time Mr. Baxter presented his latest gift, 14,286 acres in 1949, there was some complaint from sportsmen over the vast amount of land on which no hunting was permitted, but they got little response from the general public. »

Baxter State Park may be reached by three highways. These start at Millinocket, at Patten and at Greenville. It is 250 miles from Portland to the peak of Katahdin, and the nearest town to the park is twenty miles away. Sixty camps and cabins and many fireplaces have been erected along many trails, but visitors really have to rough it. Ample food supplies must be carried in if one is planning to stay more than a day, and the right kind of wilderness clothing is a necessity.

Although the present road system is limited, it will be expanded. When

Above: Pinnacle Rock on the West side of Mt. Katahdin, Baxter Park.

BILL GORMAN
« *L.L.'s wish for a larger Baxter State Park has been realized many times over the years through land acquisitions. In fact, L.L. Bean celebrated its niniety-fifth anniversary by making the lead gift of $1 million to the campaign to annex the 4,040-acre Katahdin Lake wilderness in 2008. With new land acquisition has come new rules. Today hunting (with the exception of moose hunting and hunting over bait) is permitted in 25 percent of the park. Contact the Baxter State Park Authority for more information about the areas open to hunting.*

BILL GORMAN
» *It's true Katahdin gets up early in the morning, but an analysis by Blanton C. Wiggin, published in the January 1972 issue of* Yankee *magazine, determined that the first sunrise in the U.S. actually occurs at Mars Hill in Aroostook County, Maine, for most of the spring and summer, and at Cadillac Mountain in Acadia National Park for most of the fall and winter.*

Mr. Baxter appeared before the Legislature is 1949 he agreed to allow additional road building in order that more persons could enjoy the park and that some heretofore inaccessable places of beauty might be reached.

As Mr. Baxter says, "The works of man are short lived. Monuments decay, buildings crumble, and wealth vanishes, but Katahdin in its massive grandeur will forever remain the Mountain of the People of Maine."

It is known that it is Mr. Baxter's ambition to continue adding to this great Park until it covers seven townships, making the total area 160,000 square acres. This will take out all notches shown in the map on the final pages of this book.

It is also known that Mr. Baxter has included in his will a bequest of sufficient funds to maintain it.

Mount Katahdin is the first place in the United States that is touched by the morning rays of the rising sun. «

I cannot close this chapter without mentioning the fact that Mr. Baxter recently donated his beautiful 100-acre Mackworth Island in Portland Harbor to the State of Maine.

On March 4, 1953, Mr. Baxter also gave the State $500,000.00 towards the construction of a new Home and School for the Deaf, to be built on the Island; also $210,00.00 to construct a new bridge from the Falmouth mainland to the Island.

For detail information in regard to camping, hiking and fishing, write the Baxter State Park Authority.

— CHAPTER 44 —

Bobcat Hunting

Hunting bobcats in Mid-Winter is a combination of work and fun. Walking in deep snow on snowshoes is hard, tiresome work. The $15.00 bounty paid by the State of Maine is an effort to eliminate these bloodthirsty deer killers. »

There is no closed season on cats and they are hunted about the same as coon, except coon are hunted a night, and cats in the daytime. The best time is when the snow is deep and not crusty. One or two good dogs is a "must." The dogs should be trained not to chase deer as cats are invariably found in the deer yards, near the deer they have killed.

When a track is located the dog is held in leash till the track gets very fresh, so that the cat can be treed before finding a hole in a ledge to run into. Cat hunting is a very rugged sport for able-bodied men only. »

I would advise anyone who contemplates a cat hunt to get in touch with Mr. Roy Gray, Maine Warden Supervisor, Rangeley, Maine, or the State of Maine Publicity Bureau, 3 St. John St., Portland, Maine.

BILL GORMAN
« *Today there is a debate about whether to place a bounty on coyotes. Coyotes came on the scene in Maine in the 1960s. I respect a coyote. They're beautiful, but they are savage.*

BILL GORMAN
« *Maine still has a bobcat season, and it's widely regarded as the most challenging hunt in the state. The season generally runs from early December to mid-February. There is no bag or possession limit.*

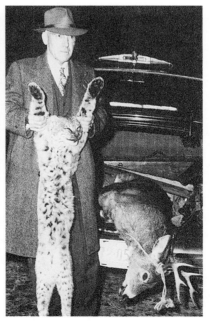

Left: This cat was killed in the deep snow with a cantdog at Solon, Maine, by Duke Adams. No doubt this cat lost one of his front legs by being caught in a trap. **Right:** Harold H. Duckett, a Freeport businessman, proudly displays a 46-pound Canadian Lynx, or bobcat, he shot on a trail in Aroostook County woods near Kingman, Fall 1951.

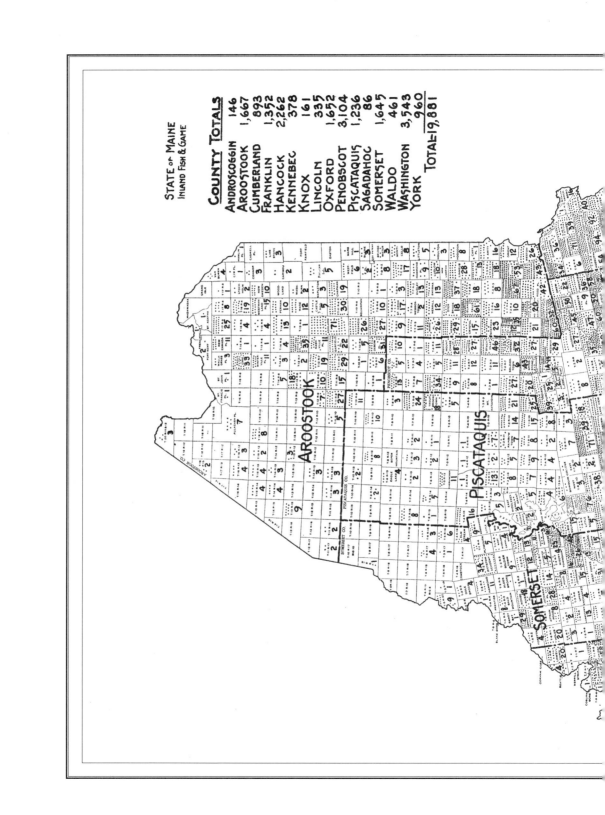

STATE OF MAINE
INLAND FISH & GAME

COUNTY TOTALS

County	Total
ANDROSCOGGIN	146
AROOSTOOK	1,667
CUMBERLAND	893
FRANKLIN	1,352
HANCOCK	2,262
KENNEBEC	378
KNOX	161
LINCOLN	335
OXFORD	1,652
PENOBSCOT	3,104
PISCATAQUIS	1,236
SAGADAHOC	86
SOMERSET	1,645
WALDO	461
WASHINGTON	3,543
YORK	960
TOTAL=	**19,881**

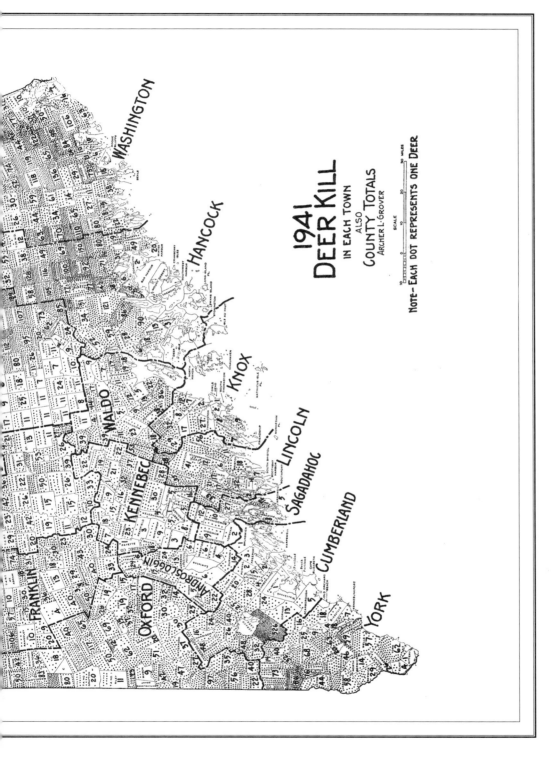

1941
DEER KILL
IN EACH TOWN
ALSO
COUNTY TOTALS
ARCHER L. GROVER

SCALE

NOTE—EACH DOT REPRESENTS ONE DEER

WASHINGTON

HANCOCK

KNOX

LINCOLN

SAGADAHOC

CUMBERLAND

YORK

WALDO

KENNEBEC

FRANKLIN

OXFORD

ANDROSCOGGIN

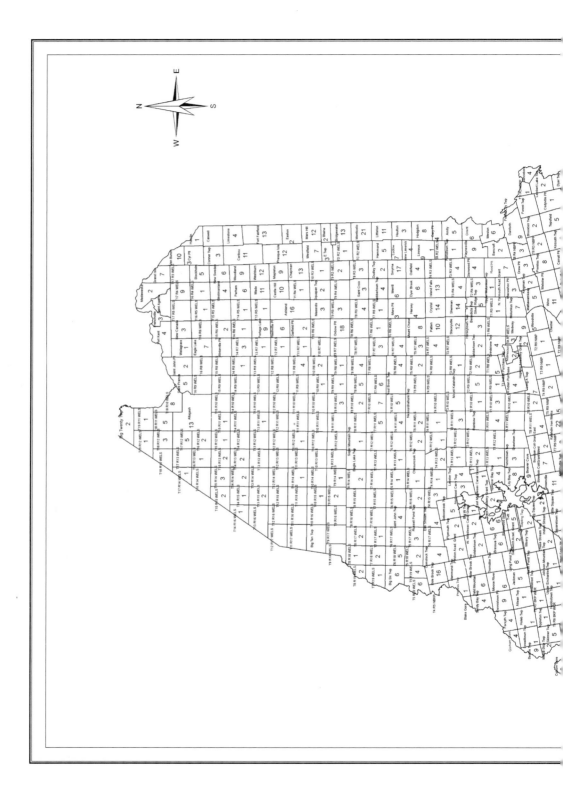

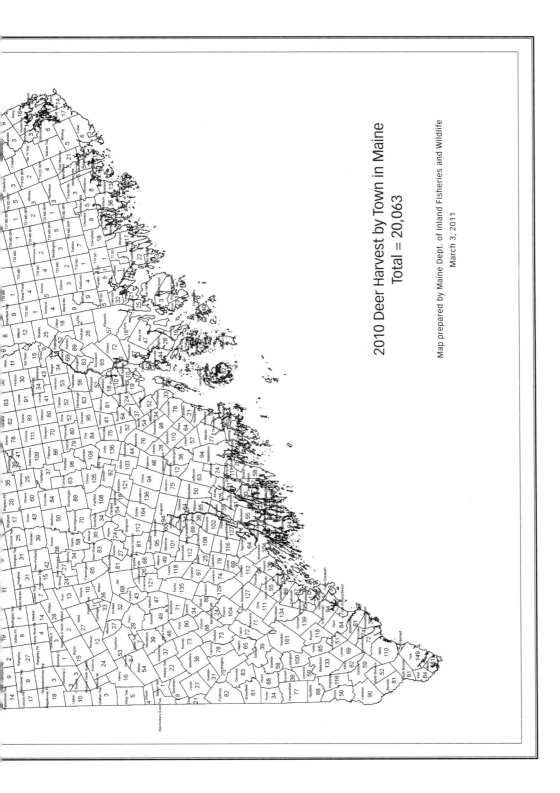

2010 Deer Harvest by Town in Maine
Total = 20,063

Map prepared by Maine Dept. of Inland Fisheries and Wildlife

March 3, 2011

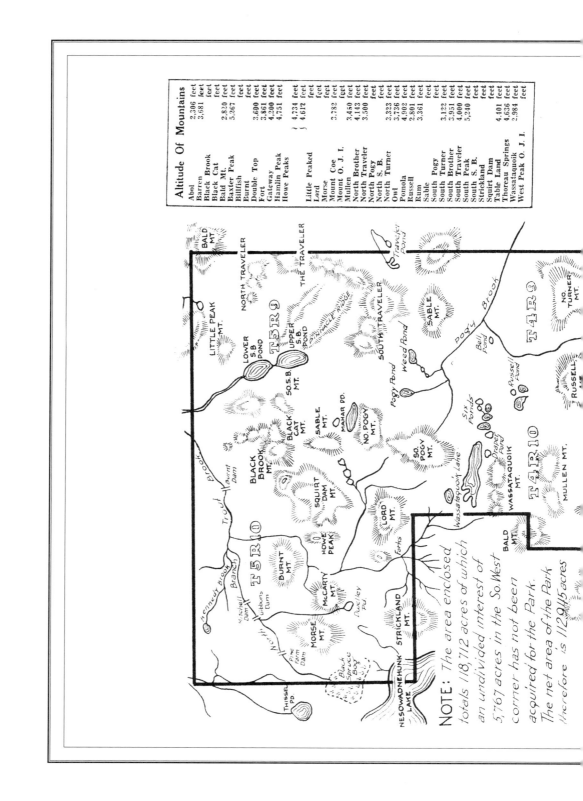

Altitude Of Mountains

Mountain	Altitude
Abol	2,306 feet
Barren	3,681 feet
Black Brook	feet
Black Cat	feet
Bald Mt.	2,820 feet
Baxter Peak	5,267 feet
Billfish	feet
Burnt	feet
Double Top	3,600 feet
Fort	3,861 feet
Gateway	4,200 feet
Hamlin Peak	4,751 feet
Howe Peaks	4,734 feet
Little Peaked	4,612 feet
Lord	feet
Morse	feet
Mount Coe	2,782 feet
Mount O. J. I.	feet
Mullen	3,450 feet
North Brother	4,143 feet
North Traveler	3,500 feet
North Pogy	feet
North S. B.	feet
North Turner	3,323 feet
Owl	3,736 feet
Pomola	4,902 feet
Russell	2,801 feet
Rum	3,361 feet
Sable	feet
South Pogy	3,122 feet
South Turner	3,951 feet
South Brother	4,000 feet
South Traveler	5,240 feet
South Peak	feet
South S. B.	feet
Strickland	feet
Squirt Dam	feet
Table Land	4,101 feet
Thoreau Springs	1,636 feet
Wassataquoik	2,984 feet
West Peak O. J. I.	feet

NOTE: The area enclosed totals 118,712 acres of which an undivided interest of 5,767 acres in the So.West corner has not been acquired for the Park. The net area of the Park therefore is 112,945 acres

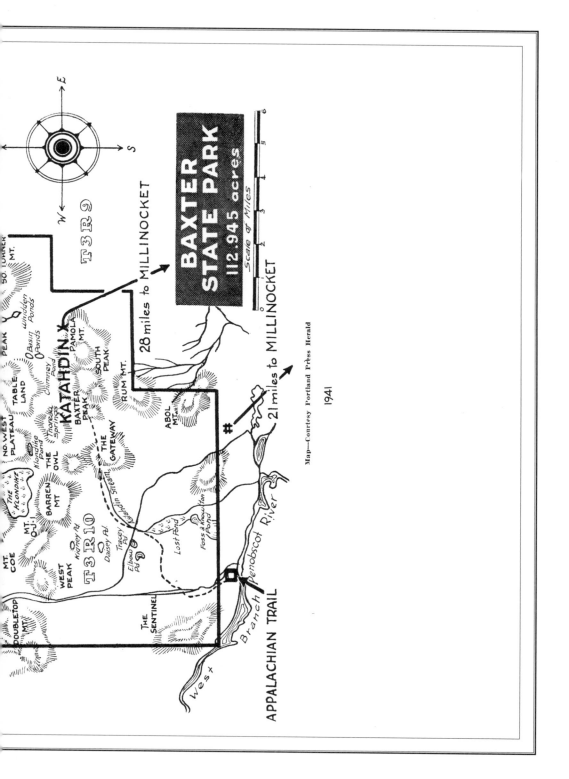

BAXTER STATE PARK
112,945 acres

28 miles to MILLINOCKET

21 miles to MILLINOCKET

APPALACHIAN TRAIL

1941

Map—Courtesy Portland Press Herald